Advance Praise for *Assessing Stude*

"Oh my, how our vision of excellence in assess
decades! McTighe and Ferrara map our collective assessment future by strongly
advising teachers and school leaders to tap profound school improvement gains
by refocusing their assessment spotlight from once a year to continuous, from
accountability testing to classroom assessment, from emphasis on selected response
to performance assessments, from grading/sorting to assessment for learning, and
from student as assessment victim to assessment partner."

—**Rick Stiggins,** Assessment Training Institute, Portland, OR

"Every classroom teacher should read this book to affirm, fine tune, or challenge
their assessment practices and decide what they will continue, what they will
start doing, and most importantly, what they will stop doing. Furthermore, at any
time that they are making assessment plans, they should refer to the three-part
assessment framework that summarizes the components of high-quality classroom assessment—assessment planning, assessment methods, and evaluation and
communication methods—because it is the best description of the three purposes
for assessment I have ever seen."

—**Ken O'Connor,** author and consultant

"Just as the pioneering work of Grant Wiggins and Jay McTighe influenced teaching practices around the world, *Assessing Student Learning by Design* will help the
next generation of educators transform standards and curriculum into engaging
assessments for learning. For veteran teachers who have grown cynical about the
never-ending onslaught of things called 'assessments,' the authors provide an essential alternative—assessments focused on student needs that are fair and accurate. For educational leaders, this book is an important consumer's guide that will
steer them away from false claims of assessments that are labeled as 'formative'
but are in fact more accurately described as uninformative. McTighe and Ferrara
give us a framework that places assessment where it belongs—as part of the daily
practice of teachers and students as they receive continuous feedback, gain understanding, and regain the joys of teaching and learning."

—**Douglas B. Reeves,** founder, Creative Leadership Solutions

"The strength and uniqueness of this concise and clearly written text is that it uses
nontechnical language to provide fundamental classroom assessment principles that
teachers and administrators across grade levels and subjects can use to effectively
personalize assessment strategies in their classrooms and schools. The internation-
ally recognized authors bring their extensive experience and expertise to show
how high-quality classroom assessment is planned, implemented, and used to both
evaluate and enhance student proficiency. Through the extensive use of reflective
questions and realistic examples, prospective and practicing teachers will learn how
to apply contemporary assessment principles. Among the key assessment strategies
presented, there is a notable emphasis on authentic performance-based assessment.
There is also a very helpful chapter for school leaders that presents strategies for improving classroom assessment. This is a book that is much needed in the education
profession to provide a solid, succinct roadmap to improved classroom assessment."

—**James McMillan,** professor emeritus, Virginia Commonwealth University

"Timely and timeless—McTighe and Ferrara understand that good assessment is simply part of good teaching. Through clear prose, sound principles, and practical examples, the authors show us how assessment in not merely about measurement. Rather, well-designed assessment practices can actually progress student learning. Now more than ever, this is a must-read resource for current and aspiring teachers and instructional leaders."

—Christopher R. Gareis, professor of education,
William & Mary School of Education

"This book is a small but mighty primer for educators of all kinds who want to understand and harness the power of classroom assessment that, as the authors say, enhances learning. Its writing is spare, clear, and accessible. Its carefully chosen analogies make important ideas relatable to readers. Its illustrations come from a broad range of subjects and grade levels. The accompanying Assessment Planning Framework guides teachers in revisiting and connecting the key aspects of assessment as they select, develop, and engage students with assessment practices. In a time when high-stakes standardized tests have become the dominant measure of student and teacher success, this book reminds readers that assessment becomes truly valuable as it improves learning."

—Carol Ann Tomlinson, William Clay Parrish Jr. Professor Emeritus,
University of Virginia School of Education and Human Development

"In *Assessing Student Learning by Design*, McTighe and Ferrara offer teachers clear and practical guidelines for developing assessments that truly inform teaching and improve student learning. What makes their book unique, however, is that instead of simply describing what to do, the authors explain why. Their book does what they want assessments of student learning to do: Encourage deeper understanding and higher levels of learning success."

—Thomas R. Guskey, professor emeritus, University of Kentucky

"In *Assessing Student Learning by Design*, Jay McTighe and Steve Ferrara outline principles and practices that promote assessment literacy by clearly defining the purposes of assessing and evaluating, and by outlining the importance of communicating results. They provide school leaders guidance on evaluating their teachers' understanding of sound assessment principles and supply strategies and resources to help promote professional learning. This is a valuable resource for educators and school leaders alike that will ultimately impact student learning."

—Kristen Maxey-Moore, North Carolina assessment program and
former assessment director in the Guilford County, NC
and Denver public school systems

Assessing Student Learning by Design

Principles and Practices for Teachers and School Leaders

Jay McTighe
Steve Ferrara

Foreword by Susan Brookhart

TEACHERS COLLEGE PRESS

TEACHERS COLLEGE | COLUMBIA UNIVERSITY
NEW YORK AND LONDON

Published by Teachers College Press,® 1234 Amsterdam Avenue, New York, NY 10027

Library of Congress Cataloging-in-Publication Data

Names: McTighe, Jay, author. | Ferrara, Steven, author.
Title: Assessing student learning by design : principles and practices for
    teachers and school leaders / Jay McTighe, Steve Ferrara.
Other titles: Assessing learning in the classroom
Description: New York : Teachers College Press, 2021. | Revised edition of:
    Assessing learning in the classroom. Washington, DC : National Education
    Association, c2000. | Includes bibliographical references and index.
Identifiers: LCCN 2020055839 (print) | LCCN 2020055840 (ebook) |
    ISBN 9780807765401 (paperback) | ISBN 9780807765418 (hardcover) |
    ISBN 9780807779590 (ebook)
Subjects: LCSH: Achievement tests—United States. | Educational tests and
    measurements—United States.
Classification: LCC LB3060.3 .M38 2021 (print) | LCC LB3060.3 (ebook) |
    DDC 371.26/2—dc23
LC record available at https://lccn.loc.gov/2020055839
LC ebook record available at https://lccn.loc.gov/2020055840

ISBN 978-0-8077-6540-1 (paper)
ISBN 978-0-8077-6541-8 (hardcover)
ISBN 978-0-8077-7959-0 (ebook)

Printed on acid-free paper
Manufactured in the United States of America

Contents

Foreword

Assessment is a life-or-death matter in the classroom. Don't take my word for it. Recently, I facilitated a session of a professional learning community (PLC) group focused on assessment. Because of the pandemic we were meeting virtually, our faces all arranged in the familiar "Hollywood Squares" display in Zoom. We had met monthly during the first semester of this school year, and the same members had participated in a similar PLC the previous year. We were focusing on formative assessment and I posed the question, "A colleague comes to you and asks why they should bother to learn and practice formative assessment in the classroom. What would you say to them?" The purpose of that exercise was to help the PLC members reflect on what they had learned—the allotted time for this PLC will end next month, so we're working on closure—and at the same time to equip these experienced teachers to share the knowledge and skills they had been developing in our PLC as they became leaders for other professional learning groups in the district, which is their next step.

Their answers blew me away. They bluntly acknowledged that, as is the case for developing any new knowledge or practices, professional development in formative assessment requires a learning curve. But after that, they were all adamant that formative assessment saves time, conserving energy for both teachers and students. Teaching becomes more precise, because teachers have clearer and more fine-grained information about what students know. Teaching becomes more aligned, because assessment requires clear understanding of what one is teaching; for example, some of the PLC members reported realizing they had over- or underemphasized a standard as they planned for assessment. Student learning increases, in both speed and amount, because students know what it is they are trying to learn and have information they can use to monitor and adjust their progress.

Although I believe everything in the previous paragraph and can cite research to support it, these thoughts are not what I said, but what the teachers in the PLC said. These were the thoughts from a professional learning community of experienced teachers who arrived at these understandings by virtue of their experience working with formative assessment and thoughtful reflection on that experience.

Another thing that blew me away was how long the group discussion ran. The participants got more insistent as the discussion progressed. My observation was that at some point fairly soon in the discussion, they realized that this was not simply a facilitation question asked by their PLC leader, but rather life-and-death stuff, meaning that if they couldn't explain to other teachers that effective assessment is a game changer in the classroom, their future work would be pointless. There was a noticeable shift in the tone of the discussion from Zoom-conference participation to real-life conversation. If they couldn't convince the teachers they were going to work with to mount the learning curve that it took to practice effective classroom assessment, those teachers would never help themselves and their students by using assessment in the way that the PLC members knew was effective and satisfying.

Which brings me to you, the reader of this foreword, and to the contents of this book. This book is about all types of effective classroom assessment, both formative and summative, but the insights of my PLC members still apply. This is life-and-death stuff—if you consider wasting teacher planning time and student time to be grave missed opportunities, little deaths in learning, as I do.

In *Assessing Student Learning by Design,* authors Jay McTighe and Steve Ferrara lay out principles and practices—that is, knowledge and skills—that teachers and school administrators need to mount the learning curve toward being an effective user of classroom assessment. It's concise and readable, full of examples, and covers all the basic principles and practices. After reading, your next step will be to practice with those elements of classroom assessment until you get good at using them. You'll know you are good at it when your professional understanding of assessment begins to resonate with the thoughts of my PLC members. In the next step after that, you might want to pursue deeper understanding of some aspect of classroom assessment that particularly interests you. Equipped with the foundational principles and practices described in this book, you will be ready to do that.

The book itself is well organized, and a look at the table of contents is all you need for understanding how it is organized. Each chapter is comprised of a set of principles, topics, practices, or tips. My advice is to read the book from front to back, because everything builds from those principles in Chapter 1. However, the nice organization laid out in the table of contents will make it easy for you to dip back into the book to refer to something as you are practicing.

Finally, I want to offer a note of appreciation to the authors themselves. Jay McTighe and Steve Ferrara have been champions of effective classroom assessment for decades, both separately and together. They are leaders in helping stakeholders at all levels (state, district, school, and classroom) and in all arenas (academic, professional, and commercial) to grow in their understanding and practice of assessment. This book is another contribution to that cause, and I'm delighted that you are reading it.

—*Susan Brookhart*

Acknowledgment

We stand on the shoulders of giants. Many of the ideas in this book were shaped by well-known and influential thinkers like Ralph Tyler, Benjamin Bloom, and Grant Wiggins. Their seminal ideas about assessment have been nurtured and enhanced by current thought leaders including Rick Stiggins, Linda Darling-Hammond, Jim MacMillan, Lorrie Shepard, Tom Guskey, Susan Brookhart, Cathy Taylor, and Dylan Wiliam. We acknowledge and celebrate their exceptional contributions to the principles and practices of classroom assessment.

Introduction

Ongoing assessment of student learning in the classroom is an essential aspect of effective teaching. Teachers can use a variety of assessment methods to diagnose students' strengths and needs, plan and adjust instruction, and provide feedback to students and parents regarding progress and achievement. The basic premise of this book is that the primary purpose of classroom assessment is to inform teaching and improve learning, not to simply justify a grade or sort and select students.

The book is intended for teachers from the preschool to graduate school levels to use in examining a variety of methods for effectively and fairly assessing their students. Educational assessment is a multidimensional process. Part of the book's title, *by design*, is meant to suggest that effective assessment results from careful planning and clarity about educational goals, various assessment purposes, diverse audiences for assessment information, types of assessment formats and tools, and options for communicating the results. Although the choice of particular assessment methods will vary according to the purpose of the assessment, the targeted learning goals, and the age levels of students, a set of common principles underlies effective classroom assessment. This book addresses these principles, examines the strengths and limitations of a variety of assessment methods, presents illustrative examples, and offers a comprehensive framework and set of guiding questions to use in planning classroom and school-level assessments to improve teaching and learning.

Teachers frequently begin new units of study by introducing or reviewing key vocabulary with the recognition that an understanding of certain basic concepts will enhance subsequent learning of important principles and procedures in the unit. Likewise, we'll begin with a review of basic terminology commonly associated with classroom assessment. *Assessment* refers to "any systematic basis for making inferences about characteristics of people, usually based on various sources of evidence; the global process of synthesizing information about individuals in order to understand and describe them better" (Brown, 1983). It is important to note that this definition contains two critical points—namely that assessment is an inferential process. Educators sometimes loosely refer to an assessment as being valid and reliable. However, a more precise conception has to do with the extent to which the results of an assessment enable valid and reliable inferences. The second point reflects the recognition that all forms of assessment are susceptible to measurement error. Accordingly, our inferences are more dependable when we consider various sources of evidence based on multiple measures.

It is interesting to note that the term *assessment* is derived from the Latin root *assidere*, meaning "to sit beside." Although this original meaning may seem at odds with images of standardized testing, multiple-choice "bubble" sheets, rigid time limits, and silent work, it conforms more closely with the array of assessment methods routinely used by teachers for assessing their students. Indeed, *assidere* suggests that in addition to tests and performance assessments, classroom assessments include informal methods of "sitting beside"—observing, and conversing with students—as a means of understanding and describing what they know and can do.

The terms *assessment, testing,* and *evaluation* are frequently used interchangeably, but they have distinct meanings. *Assessment,* as defined above, is a broad term referring to the process of gathering and synthesizing information to better understand and describe learning. *Testing* is one type of assessment. Tests generally utilize a paper-and-pencil or computer-based format, are administered and taken within established time limits, restrict test takers' access to resources (e.g., reference materials), and yield a limited range of acceptable responses. *Evaluation* refers to the process of making a judgment regarding the degree of knowledge, understanding, skill proficiency, or product/ performance quality based on established criteria and performance standards.

Another pair of widely used terms, *summative assessment* and *formative assessment,* pertain to the purpose and timing of classroom assessments. *Summative assessment* generally refers to any culminating assessment that provides a summary report on the degree of knowledge or proficiency attained at the conclusion of a unit, course, or program of study. However, we prefer to use the term *evaluative assessment* for those measures that result in a final score or grade. Scoring a student essay against a rubric and assigning report card grades are examples, as is a final exam, senior exhibition, or dissertation defense.

We distinguish evaluative assessments from *formative assessments* that are used in conjunction with instruction to provide feedback to teachers and students about the learning process. For example, teachers often use classroom questions and brief written checks to determine if students are learning targeted material and can apply the skills being taught. Teachers use the results of such ongoing assessments to provide students with feedback that can help them improve, such as when they return draft work with comments and suggestions. Formative assessments also provide teachers with valuable information about how they may need to adjust or differentiate their instruction to improve student performance.

Diagnostic assessment (sometimes known as preassessments) are employed prior to a new unit of instruction or course to help teachers gauge students' prior knowledge and skill levels in order to determine the optimal starting place for new instruction. For instance, prior to the start of a unit on the Civil War, a teacher might ask students to make a "web" or an outline to show what they already know about this period of history. The teacher might also randomly select and interview several students to check their awareness of the Civil War and whether they have any misconceptions.

In addition to these fundamental assessment terms, we will introduce additional terminology throughout the book and offer a more complete set of definitions in the Glossary.

Thank you for investing your time in reading our book. We trust that its ideas will deepen your understanding of the principles of effective assessment and enhance your assessment practices in the classroom.

—Jay and Steve

CHAPTER 1

Principles of Effective Classroom Assessment

Assessment is the bridge between teaching and learning. Indeed, anyone interested in either should also be interested in assessment. It is one thing to say I taught something; it is quite another to ask, what did my students gain from my teaching? To what extent do they understand this new concept? How proficient are they with this skill? Do they harbor any misconceptions about the content? Well-designed classroom assessments help us answer these critical questions. The results of our assessments can provide invaluable feedback to help us know the effect of our teaching and to guide future instruction. Assessments also provide information for students about what they have learned well and about areas needing improvement.

To be most effective, classroom assessment should be grounded by sound principles (McTighe, 2013; McTighe & Ferrara, 1998). In this chapter, we offer five principles to guide your assessment practices and make it more likely that your teaching will be most impactful and student learning will be maximized:

1. Assessments should serve learning.
2. Multiple measures provide more evidence.
3. Assessments should align with goals.
4. Assessments should measure what matters.
5. Assessments should be fair.

PRINCIPLE 1: ASSESSMENT SHOULD SERVE LEARNING

The first principle asserts that the primary purpose of classroom assessment is to inform teaching and improve learning. To say that assessment should serve learning is a nice slogan with which people are likely to agree. But what exactly does it mean? This principle suggests that assessment be viewed as an ongoing process instead of a single event at the conclusion of an instructional segment. Rather than waiting until the end of a unit or course to assess students' learning, effective teachers employ preassessments at the beginning of instruction to determine students' prior knowledge and skill levels, and they assess regularly throughout the unit or course to help them adjust their teaching based on the learning needs of students. They recognize that assessment results provide more than just data for grading students; assessments provide feedback as the fuel for improving teaching and learning.

To explore the impact of assessment practices that can inform teaching and improve learning, Wiggins and McTighe developed and used a workshop exercise to inductively explore this assessment principle (McTighe, 2018). They asked people to think of a highly effective learning experience in their lives and to then identify ways in which the assessments, and how the results were used, contributed to that learning. The responses to the exercise are remarkably similar across groups. Here is a representative list of the characteristics of assessment practices that contribute to deep and effective learning (McTighe, 2018):

Assessments enhance learning when:

- The "end" learning goals are known in advance, as are the assessments of them.
- The criteria for success are presented and explained at the beginning.
- Models of excellence, aligned to the criteria, are shown to provide a clear picture of desired performance.
- The assessment tasks are set in a realistic context and required application (i.e., authentic, performance-based).
- The assessments are challenging yet attainable.
- The assessments are "open" (i.e., there was not a single correct answer or a single way of accomplishing the task).
- Students produced tangible products and/or performance to show evidence of their learning.
- There is often an audience other than the teacher–instructor.
- The learners have some choice regarding how they could demonstrate their learning (e.g., via products and performances) and/or how they went about the task (process).

- There are often the opportunities to work with others (collaboration).
- The teacher–instructor functions like a coach or an advocate (i.e., a critical friend, not an adversary).
- Detailed feedback is provided along the way.
- Learners have opportunities to practice, refine, or redo after feedback is given.
- Learners are encouraged to reflect on their learning and set future goals based on the assessment results.

By emulating these features, our classroom assessment practices can contribute to learning, not just measure it.

PRINCIPLE 2: MULTIPLE MEASURES PROVIDE MORE EVIDENCE

Assessment is a process by which we make inferences about what students know, understand, and can do based on information obtained through assessments. Educators sometimes loosely refer to an assessment as being valid and reliable. However, a more precise conception has to do with the extent to which the results of an assessment enable valid and reliable inferences. Since all forms of assessment are susceptible to measurement error, our inferences are more dependable when we consider multiple measures (i.e., various sources of evidence). Psychometricians (professional measurement specialists, like Steve) understand this basic assessment principle and, in fact, most commercial standardized tests include related disclaimers. This point is reaffirmed in "A Guide for Effective Assessment" from CTB/McGraw-Hill (2010):

> No single test can do it all. A diagnostic test to determine the emission level of an automobile engine will not tell you that the tires need air. A different procedure is needed to provide that information. The same goes for tests in education. No single test can ascertain whether all educational goals are being met. A variety of tests, or "multiple measures," is necessary to tell educators what students know and can do. And just as different tests provide different information, no one test can tell us all we need to know about one student's progress.

Consider this principle in terms of a photographic analogy. A photo album typically contains a number of pictures taken over time in different contexts. When viewed as a whole, the album presents a more accurate and revealing portrait of an individual than does any single snapshot. Indeed, some photographs, like a candid photo that captures an unflattering expression or one taken on a "bad hair" day, would actually present a distorted picture if viewed in isolation. However, when one views a number of pictures together, the effect of one or two outliers will be offset by other pictures that offer a truer rendition of a subject.

At the classroom level, a single assessment is like a snapshot in that it provides a picture of student learning at a single moment in time. It would be inappropriate to use a single assessment as the sole basis for drawing conclusions about how well a student has achieved an important learning outcome. The multiple measures principle suggests that we think of classroom assessment akin to the assembly of a photo album containing a variety of pictures taken at different times with different lenses, backgrounds, and compositions. Such an album offers a richer, fairer, and more complete picture of student achievement than any single snapshot can provide. Applying the principle of multiple sources is especially important when the assessment information is used for important evaluative decisions, such as assigning report card grades.

PRINCIPLE 3: ASSESSMENTS SHOULD ALIGN WITH LEARNING GOALS

To enable valid inferences to be drawn from the results, an assessment must provide an appropriate measure of a given learning goal. Since teachers typically direct their instruction toward different types of goals, we need an associated variety of assessments in order to gather the appropriate evidence for *all* targeted goals. To extend the photographic analogy, a diversity of educational goals implies that we should include a variety of pictures in our assessment photo album. For example, if we want to see if students know multiplication tables or chemical symbols, then objective test items—such as multiple-choice, matching, true–false, or fill-in-the-blank—will provide the appropriate evidence in an efficient manner. When we wish to check for proficiency in skill–process areas such as drawing, writing, or a skill in physical education, some type of performance assessment is needed. For dispositional goals, such as open-mindness or persistence, evidence will have to be collected over time through observations and self-assessments. We will discuss different types of learning goals and various forms of assessment in subsequent chapters.

Principle 3 addresses the concept of validity—that is, the extent to which an assessment measures what it was intended to measure. In his classic book *Educative Assessment*, Grant Wiggins (1998) proposed a two-question test to check for validity:

1. Could a student pass your test or perform the task in a way that meets your performance standard, yet not effectively demonstrate the targeted knowledge, understanding, and/or skill proficiency?
2. Could a student do poorly on your test or not meet your performance standard, yet have nonetheless attained the targeted knowledge, understanding, and/or skill proficiency?

If the answer to either question is yes, then the assessment does not yet provide a valid measure of the specified learning outcomes.

Despite the importance of collecting multiple pieces of evidence and matching the measures with goals, we often observe teachers making assessment decisions based on what is easiest to test and grade. Although this is understandable given the time- and labor-intensiveness of some types of assessments, and the pressure to "defend" grades to students, parents, and administrators, we nonetheless advocate that our goals should dictate the nature of our assessments, not external factors. It is incumbent on school and district leaders to establish structures (such as time for group scoring of student work and realistic grade-completion timelines) so that valid assessment practices can be implemented feasibly.

Here is a quick and practical way of checking the alignment between your assessments and your identified learning goals (McTighe, 2013). First, develop a draft unit that includes the standards or learning outcomes that you want students to attain. Then, specify the assessments you plan to use to determine if the targeted learning has been achieved. (Note: You do not need to include lesson plans.) Now, show your proposed unit assessments to another teacher or team, and ask them to infer what they believe the standards or outcomes to be based *only* on your assessments. If they can determine all of your targeted goals, then you have validation that your assessments are likely to provide valid measures. If they can infer some, but not all, of your outcomes, then you will likely need to add or modify one or more of your assessments (or eliminate one or more of your goals since they are not being assessed).

This alignment check can be done informally with a colleague, or during a faculty or team meeting. Jay has found that after teachers do this once or twice, they find themselves thinking much more carefully about the alignment between their learning goals and the needed assessment evidence.

PRINCIPLE 4: ASSESSMENTS SHOULD MEASURE WHAT MATTERS

You've no doubt heard aphorisms such as, "We measure what we value," "What gets measured is what gets done," or "It only counts if it counts." Indeed, what we assess sends strong messages to students about what learning outcomes are valued. Learners are quick to pick up on this as they move through school. "Will this count?" is an irritatingly familiar student query, and they quickly conclude that if a teacher does not assess something, "it doesn't really matter."

This educational truism raises a crucial question: Are we assessing all valued learning outcomes or only those things that are easiest to test and grade? In large-scale, standardized assessments, the answer is clearly no. For example, virtually all Standards in English/Language Arts include listening and speaking, and these are recognized as the foundations of literacy and the underpinnings of reading and writing. Yet listening and speaking are rarely, if ever, assessed on standardized accountability tests. Indeed, most standardized tests do not assess other goals that matter in a modern education because they are more challenging and expensive to measure in a large scale.

However, the fact that such outcomes are not assessed on standardized tests should *not* mean that they are unimportant and can be omitted from classroom assessments. To the contrary, the classroom is the ideal setting for using a range of assessments that can provide both formative feedback and evaluative evidence for a range of vital learning goals, including scientific investigation, historical inquiry, research, argumentation, multimedia communication, creative design, and the ability to collaborate in teams. We will discuss the use of varied assessment methods to gather evidence on a broad range of learning goals in subsequent chapters. In the meantime, ask yourself: Are any valued outcomes in your classroom or school "falling through the cracks" because they are not being assessed?

PRINCIPLE 5: ASSESSMENTS SHOULD BE FAIR

The principle of fairness in classroom assessment simply means giving all students an equal chance to show what they know, understand, and can do. Fairness for large-scale achievement tests is provided by standardization; that is, the items, conditions for administering the test (e.g., strict time limits), and the scoring procedures are typically standardized; that is, the same for all students. Standardized assessments enable comparability and are also intended to be fair since all students are assessed in an identical manner.

However, another aspect of fairness has to do with enabling learners to demonstrate their learning in an appropriate manner. A student who has reading difficulties or is not fluent in English may not understand a written test question or the task directions, even though they might understand the tested content. In such cases, a one-size-fits-all assessment would not be a fair representation of their learning. Of course, large-scale, accountability tests typically allow specified accommodations for test takers with disabilities and language limitations who need them—for example, presenting items in large type or orally for students who are visually impaired.

Classroom assessments are less constrained by the technical demands for consistency and comparability than external, standardized tests. Thus, teachers can be more flexible in their efforts to ensure that their assessments are fair to all students. For example, learners may be enabled to show their mastery of a social studies concept by presenting a graphic organizer or offering an oral explanation instead of only through a written response. In some cases, it may be appropriate to allow certain students more time to complete a task. When allowing variations in an assessment, it is nonetheless important to honor the alignment principle. In other words, the assessment options must still provide appropriate evidence of the targeted learning outcomes. If not, then you could be assessing apples versus oranges.

The fairness of an assessment can also be compromised as a result of unintended racial, ethnic, religious, or gender biases. For example, insensitivity to diverse religious beliefs (e.g., choosing reading passages involving only Christian holidays), gender roles or racial images (e.g., depicting all doctors as White males), or socioeconomic status (e.g., assuming that all kids have access to the Internet or a smartphone) may negatively influence students' attitudes toward, and performances on, classroom assessments.

CONCLUSION

These five principles function like a rudder underneath a ship—they help you stay on course to ensure that your classroom assessments will provide the evidence you need to support student learning. In the next chapter, we move from principle to practice and present an assessment-planning framework.

Reflection Questions

- What specific assessment practices do you employ in your classroom that reflect one or more of the five principles that we present in this chapter?
- What changes in assessment practices in your classroom or school would bring them in greater accord with one or more of the five principles?

CHAPTER 2

An Assessment-Planning Framework

Any trustworthy educational assessment should begin with a consideration of three interrelated factors: the targeted learning goals, the purpose(s) for assessment, and the audience(s) for the resulting information. These factors can be considered as questions: (1) *What are the targeted learning goals, and how are they best assessed?* (2) *What is the purpose(s) of the assessment?* and (3) *For whom are the assessment results intended, and how will those results be used?* The answers to these questions will guide your decisions, including what kinds of assessment methods to use and how to best communicate their results.

The assessment-planning framework presented in Figures 2.1, 2.2, and 2.3 can assist educators in planning assessments at the classroom, school, and district levels (adapted from McTighe & Ferrara, 1998). This framework is organized around key questions and offers a set of options for consideration. In this chapter we'll explore the first section of this framework, while subsequent chapters will examine the second and third sections in greater detail.

BEGIN WITH THE END IN MIND

First and foremost, planning appropriate assessments begins with clarity about the learning goals we seek. We propose that there are categorically four distinct types of learning goals, and each of these calls for particular kinds of assessment evidence and, therefore, is best assessed with different assessment methods. These four goal categories are listed in the first column of page one of the assessment-planning framework (Figure 2.1).

Let's examine each of the four goal types and consider their implications for assessment.

Figure 2.1. Assessment-Planning Framework: Key Questions

Desired Learning Results	Purpose(s) for Assessment	Audience(s) for Assessment
What do we want students to know, understand, be able to do, and be like?	*Why are we assessing? How will the assessment information be used?*	*For whom are the assessment results intended? What information is needed?*

Knowledge:
•
•
•
•
 	
Skills and processes:
•
•
•
 	
Understandings:
•
•
•
•
 	
Dispositions:
•
•
•
•
	❑ diagnose student strengths and needs
	❑ provide feedback on student learning
	❑ provide a basis for instructional placement
	❑ inform and guide instruction
	❑ communicate learning expectations
	❑ motivate; focus student attention and effort
	❑ provide practice applying knowledge and skills
	❑ provide a basis for evaluation
	   • grading
	   • promotion/graduation
	   • program selection/admission
	❑ provide accountability data
	❑ school/district
	❑ teachers/administrators
		❑ teacher–instructor
		❑ students
		❑ parents
		❑ grade level/department team
		❑ other faculty
		❑ school administrators
		❑ curriculum supervisors
		❑ policymakers
		❑ business community/employers
		❑ college admissions officers
		❑ higher education
		❑ general public
		❑ other:

© 2020 Jay McTighe and Steve Ferrara; adapted from McTighe and Ferrara (1998). *Assessing Learning in the Classroom*. Washington, DC: National Education Association.

Knowledge

Knowledge goals specify what we want students to know. This category focuses on declarative knowledge of factual information (e.g., state capitals, multiplication tables), vocabulary terms, and basic concepts (e.g., fiction vs. nonfiction). Assessment evidence on the attainment of knowledge can be determined in a straightforward manner using objective test/quiz items or through teacher questioning. Typically, assessments of knowledge goals have a correct answer. Indeed, the assessment of knowledge is essentially a binary proposition—you either know something or you don't!

Skill and Processes

Skill and process goals state what students should be able to do. These goals are procedural in nature (i.e., they involve know-how). Some skills involve discrete and relatively simple actions, even though they may take time and effort to master. Examples of skills include drawing basic shapes, dribbling a basketball, or diagramming sentences.

Process goals typically involve more complex actions requiring multiple steps and the integration of multiple skills with declarative knowledge. The latest generation of national subject area standards prominently include such processes—for example, the Common Core State Standard (CCSS) Anchor Standards for English/Language Arts; Next Generation Science Standards (NGSS) Science and Engineering Practices (2013); the College, Career, and Civic Life (C3) Framework for Social Studies State Standards (2013); and the creative processes listed in the National Core Arts Standards (2014). Examples of such complex processes include extended writing, argumentation, scientific experimentation, literary interpretation, problem solving, and design thinking. Beyond the complex processes associated with particular disciplines (e.g., historical inquiry), a number of states and school districts have identified transdisciplinary processes, often known as 21st-century skills (e.g., critical thinking, creativity, collaboration, communication, technology use), that teachers are expected to infuse.

The proper assessment of skills and processes requires the learner to perform the skill or process in order to demonstrate their competence. Thus, skills and processes are most appropriately assessed by a learner's performance using methods such as direct observation (e.g., a skill in physical education) or an after-the-fact examination of a product or performance (e.g., assessing a writing sample or a drawing). For certain discrete skills, such as performing a basic arithmetic operation, selected or brief constructed-response test items can yield appropriate evidence. Other skills, especially those that are physical in nature (e.g., drawing a figure, playing a note on a musical instrument, parallel parking a car) are best assessed through demonstrated performance. Unlike assessment of knowledge, for which there is usually a single "right" answer, the assessment of skills and complex processes are best assessed using performance-based measures. Moreover, student performance should be conceived along a continuum of proficiency from novice to expert—think of Red Cross swimming levels or different-colored belts in martial arts as representing various performance levels. Indeed, for many of the most valued disciplinary processes, including research, argumentation, multimedia communication, literary or historical interpretation, experimental inquiry and cooperative work in a group, performance-based assessments will provide the most appropriate evidence of student proficiency levels.

Understanding

Understanding goals refer to the big ideas that we want students to comprehend at a deep level. Such ideas are inherently abstract and are stated as concepts (e.g., justice), principles (e.g., $F = MA$), and generalizations (e.g., *writers adjust their style based on their purpose and audience*). Examples of such understandings are seen in one dimension of the NGSS-cross-cutting concepts framed as understanding goals, for example:

- *Structure and function.* The way in which an object or living thing is shaped and its substructure determine many of its properties and functions.

Although multiple-choice or fill-in-the-blank test items may reveal some degree of understanding (or lack thereof) of basic concepts, we propose that the most appropriate assessments of understanding are performance based (Wiggins & McTighe, 2005, 2011, 2012). More specifically, students show evidence of their understanding when they can effectively do two things: (1) *apply* their learning, and (2) *explain* their thinking and support their responses to test items. Ultimately, assessment of understanding calls for some demonstration of transfer (i.e., using knowledge in new situations). For example, if you fully understand certain mathematical concepts and algorithms, you can use them to solve a problem that you have never seen before. This represents a qualitatively different level of performance than merely plugging numbers into a memorized algorithm or selecting the right answer from a set of given alternatives. Like a doctoral student defending a dissertation, the learner demonstrates real understanding when they can:

- Give the "why," not just the "what."
- Explain an abstract concept in their own words.
- Effectively teach someone else.
- Use new examples to illustrate a principle.
- Justify their conclusion.
- Defend their position against critique.

Dispositions

Dispositional goals, also known as *habits of mind,* highlight productive ways of thinking and acting, inside and outside of school. Art Costa and Bena Kallick (2008) have identified 16 habits of mind that they contend are vital in both school and life, including *open-mindedness, managing impulsivity,* and *listening with empathy.* Parents, teachers, and employers recognize the value of such habits, and an inclusive educational experience helps young people develop them.

A related type of dispositional goal can be found in the mission statements of independent, international, religious, and charter schools. In fact, such schools often distinguish themselves from traditional public schools by their espoused ideals (e.g., service to community, stewardship of the environment, embodiment of the arts, fostering cross-cultural understandings, and religious values).

Social and emotional learning (SEL) goals also fall into the dispositional goal category and are being pursued by schools and districts around the world. SEL goals include the abilities to "manage emotions and achieve personal and collective goals, feel and show empathy for others, establish and maintain supportive relationships, and make responsible and caring decisions" (see the Collaborative for Academic, Social, and Emotional Learning [CASEL] at https://casel.org/what-is-sel).

Although knowledge and skills can be appropriately assessed through on-demand assessments, it would be inappropriate and unnatural to have a test of *open-mindedness* or *honesty*! Indeed, the assessment of dispositional goals calls for qualitatively different approaches—for example, observations over time based on a set of observable indicators of the targeted disposition. To invoke the photographic analogy again, if traditional assessments provide moment-in-time "snapshots" of learning, then the assessment of dispositions is best accomplished with a video camera that operates over time. In other words, we look for evidence of various habits of mind appropriately applied in varied circumstances. Moreover, we would include self-assessments by the learner since a long-term goal is for students to internalize these productive habits of mind.

CLASSROOM ASSESSMENT AND NATIONAL CONTENT STANDARDS

For many teachers, learning goals have been dictated, at least in part, by standards established at the national, state, and/or district levels. It is worthwhile noting that the four types of learning goals we described can be used as a means of "unpacking" established standards. Doing so is valuable because these different goal types call for different approaches to both instruction and assessment. In fact, current versions of national and associated state content standards in various disciplines contain the first three goal types explicitly. Figure 2.2 presents examples of these various goal types found in national standards (which often serve as the basis for state standards).

Although dispositional goals are not as prominent, several of the disciplinary standards include them explicitly. For example, the Common Core Practice Standards in Mathematics (2010) highlight *perseverance* by noting that mathematically proficient students "make sense of problems and persevere in solving them." The National Core Arts Standards (2014) cite *creativity* as a valued work habit in the arts.

Beyond those listed in standards, many teachers value and encourage students to develop productive dispositions such as flexible thinking, open-mindedness, empathy for others, and willingness to accept feedback.

In sum, clarity about the learning goals, and their differences, is essential to selecting appropriate assessment measures and using their results to both communicate and advance learning in the classroom.

PURPOSE AND AUDIENCE MATTER

The second and third columns of the framework (Figure 2.1) present varied purposes and audiences to be considered. Experienced writers understand that purpose and audience matter, and they adjust their

Figure 2.2. Examples of Goal Types Found in National Content Standards

Standards	Knowledge	Skills and Processes	Understandings
Common Core State Standards—Mathematics	Use place value understanding to round whole numbers to the nearest 10 or 100. 3.NBT.A.1	Fluently divide multidigit numbers using the standard algorithm. 6.NS.B.2 Practice standard MP1. Make sense of problems and persevere in solving them.	Understand that positive and negative numbers are used together to describe quantities having opposite directions or values (e.g., temperature above/below zero, elevation above/below sea level, credits/debits, positive/negative electric charge). 6.NS.C.5
Common Core State Standards—English/ Language Arts	ELA Literacy standard By the end of the year, read and comprehend literary nonfiction in the grades 6–8 text complexity band proficiently, with scaffolding as needed at the high end of the range. RI.6.10	College and Career Readiness Anchor Standards for Reading #1—Read closely to determine what the text says explicitly and to make logical inferences from it; cite specific textual evidence when writing or speaking to support conclusions drawn from the text.	ELA Literacy standard Determine a central idea of a text and how it is conveyed through particular details; provide a summary of the text distinct from personal opinions or judgments. RI.6.2

(continued)

Figure 2.2. (continued)

Standards	Knowledge	Skills and Processes	Understandings
Next Generation Science Standards (NGSS)	Disciplinary Core Idea Weather and Climate describes patterns of typical weather conditions over different scales and variations. Historical weather patterns can be analyzed. ESS2.D	Science Practice Standard #3—Planning and carrying out investigations.	Cross-Cutting Concept #6—Structure and Function The way in which an object or living thing is shaped and its substructure determine many of its properties and functions.
The College, Career, and Civic Life (C3) Framework for Social Studies Standards	Identify different kinds of historical sources. D2.History 1.k-2	Construct maps and other graphic representations of both familiar and unfamiliar places.	Analyze ideas and principles contained in the founding documents of the United States, and explain how they influence the social and political system. D2.Civics 9.6-8
National Core Arts Standards (NCAS)	Understand that people from different places and times have made art for a variety of reasons. Visual Arts: Cn11.1.1a	Cooperate as a creative team to make interpretive choices for a drama/theater work. Theater: Cr2-11	Demonstrate an understanding of how the structure and the elements of music are used in music selected for performance. Music: Pr4.2.6

organization, style, and tone according to their intended outcomes and readers. Similarly, educators planning assessments need to be mindful of their purpose(s) and audience(s) and tailor their assessments accordingly. For example, a teacher may use a preassessment at the start of a new unit to check on students' prior knowledge and skill levels in order to target their teaching and plan for any differentiated instruction that may be necessary. In this case, the assessment results are primarily for their own use and would not be reported to others.

Alternatively, a principal might use a summary of students' grades—based on evaluative assessments—to analyze the achievement trends of various cohort groups in the school and present these in a report to the superintendent and school board.

McTighe and Wiggins (2004) propose that there are three primary purposes for classroom assessments, summarized in Figure 2.3. Assessment expert Rick Stiggins (2004) characterizes these different

Figure 2.3. Three Purposes for Classroom Assessments

Assessments for Learning		Assessment of Learning
Diagnostic	*Formative*	*Evaluative*
Assessments that precede new instruction to check students' prior knowledge and experience, possible misconceptions, and/or interests. Diagnostic assessments (also known as pre-assessments) provide information to assist teacher planning and guide differentiated instruction that may be needed.	Ongoing assessments that provide feedback to both students and teachers for the purpose of improving learning and performance. Formative assessments can include both formal (e.g., a weekly quiz) and informal methods (e.g., an observation as students work). Since their primary purpose is to provide feedback, formative assessments should not be graded.	Assessments used to determine the degree of mastery or proficiency based on identified learning goals. Evaluative assessments generally result in a score or a grade. *Note:* Some educators refer to these as summative assessments. We prefer to use the term *evaluative*, since it more directly describes their purpose.
Examples: pretest, skills check, survey, K-W-L chart	*Examples:* quiz, oral questioning, observation, draft work, "think aloud," exit card, dress rehearsal, scrimmage	*Examples:* test, final exam, performance task, culminating project, work portfolio

classroom assessment purposes as assessments *for* learning and assessments *of* learning.

CLASSROOM ASSESSMENT AND STATEWIDE ACCOUNTABILITY TESTING

Different types of assessments address different information needs. The purposes and audiences for assessment information influence what is assessed, how it is assessed, and how the results are communicated and used. Statewide accountability assessments—familiar to public school teachers, administrators, and parents in the United States—have very specific purposes and are administered using standardized procedures. Standardization of administration and scoring, plus test administration accommodations for students with disabilities and English learners who need them, are meant to ensure that all students are assessed under uniform and fair conditions so that interpretation of their performance is comparable and not influenced by differing circumstances or impediments to performance (see the Standards for Educational and Psychological Testing, 2014).

At the present time, educational accountability is determined primarily by the results of these annual standardized tests in reading, mathematics, and science administered at the state level. Standardized state accountability tests enable comparability among schools, districts, and states to identify which schools need to "raise the bar" for expected achievement. Disaggregating data from assessment results reveal disparities in achievement among subgroups of students that remain hidden if that same data were reported only for all students.

Other well-known standardized tests are used for admission into colleges and universities—for example, SAT and Advanced Placement (AP) Tests from the College Board, and the exams of the International Baccalaureate (IB). Another widely used college admissions test, the ACT, makes its fundamental purpose crystal clear:

> The ACT Test is a curriculum- and standards-based educational and career planning tool that assesses students' academic readiness for college (http://www.act.org/products/k-12-act-test/).

Thus, these tests have special relevance for students, parents, and institutions of higher education. School boards, teachers, and administrators pay close attention to their results as well.

Since large-scale, standardized tests are administered to hundreds of thousands of students, most employ a selected-response format to enable fast and relatively inexpensive machine scoring. (Note: Some large-scale tests also use brief, constructed-response items and may include essay prompts for writing.) State accountability assessments are often referred to as high-stakes tests since their results have consequences and may be used to evaluate schools and districts, impact funding levels, evaluate teachers and administrators, and in some cases, inform decisions regarding promotion or graduation of students. Public schools consume a considerable amount of public funds, and taxpayers and policymakers have a right to know how the schools are performing on behalf of students. Thus, there is a place for such external assessments as part of a comprehensive assessment system (Brookhart et al., 2019).

Although statewide accountability tests occupy a prominent place in the educational landscape, their limitations are recognized. For example, they assess only a portion of all the goals in established standards, even as other worthwhile educational goals identified in the standards are not assessed. Selected-response and brief-constructed response items are simply incapable of fully measuring students' abilities to address open-ended problems and issues, engage in discussion and debate, write for genuine audiences and purposes, conduct sound research and experimental inquiry, and engage in artistic expression. Furthermore, the so-called 21st-century skills of critical thinking, collaborative teamwork, multimedia communication, and use of information technologies are typically not tested on today's accountability measures, yet these are surely vital outcomes for a modern education (McTighe, 2018a).

Although standardized tests are limited by their scale, costs, constrained time frames, and the need to produce comparable measures at relatively low cost, classroom assessment are not similarly constrained. Teachers have multiple opportunities to assess all important learning goals, as well as to use classroom assessment diagnostically and for feedback, not just for evaluation and grading.

CONCLUSION

With clarity about the various types of learning goals and the purposes and audiences for assessment, we now turn our attention to examining specific types of classroom assessments. In the next chapter, we describe five different assessment formats and highlight their respective strengths and limitations for use in the classroom.

Reflection Questions

- How do you currently use diagnostic, formative, and evaluative assessments in your classroom?
- What is the influence of standardized accountability tests on your teaching and on your classroom assessments?
- Are you and your colleagues currently assessing *all* valued learning goals or primarily those goals that are easiest to test and grade? Are any important learning goals "falling through the cracks" because they are not being assessed?

CHAPTER 3

Assessment Methods

Once teachers identify the learning goals and determine the purposes and audiences for their assessments, they are ready to select the specific methods they will use to gather evidence of learning. The second page of our assessment-planning framework (Figure 3.1) provides five assessment formats. In this chapter, we will discuss these formats, consider the strengths and limitations of each, and offer illustrative classroom examples of how they can be used.

SELECTED RESPONSE

Selected-response formats—multiple-choice, true-false, matching, and enhanced multiple-choice items—are widely known and used in educational testing, especially at the secondary and postsecondary levels (Stiggins & Conklin, 1992). Multiple-choice items are the most common type of selected responses, appearing on statewide assessments and most commercially produced tests, as well as on many classroom assessments. The selected-response format presents students with a question, problem, or prompt followed by a set of alternative responses. Students choose from among the given alternatives rather than generate their own response. Although most selected-response items have a single correct or acceptable response, it is possible to create multiselect multiple-choice items that have more than one acceptable answer contained among the alternatives. For example:

Which *two* pairs of fractions are correct comparisons:

a. $1/3 = 2/6$
b. $1/3 < 1/4$
c. $1/3 < 3/10$

    d. $2/3 < 5/6$
    e. $3 = 8/12$
    f. $2/3 < 9/15$

You may also have seen, or used, technology-enhanced items, which enable additional response options, such as drag and drop, highlightable text, and graphing. In the case of graphing, students are asked to complete a graph in numerous ways, such as adding points and lines and writing an equation that is plotted on the graph.

Selected-response formats have a number of advantages. They enable teachers to efficiently and objectively assess students' knowledge of factual information, concepts, and the application of basic skills. Because assessments using this format can accommodate a larger number of items, they enable a teacher to sample a broad range of knowledge and skills in a limited amount of time. Since selected-response items are constructed to include correct or acceptable responses, they are easily and objectively scored as correct or incorrect using an answer key. Machine-scorable answer sheets and hand-scoring templates simplify the scoring process, enabling teachers to quickly obtain results for timely feedback. Figure 3.2 presents examples of classroom assessments using selected-response formats. Notice that these examples reflect different purposes and audiences.

Despite their advantages, assessments using selected-response formats have limitations. Instead of assessing the application of knowledge and higher-order skills in meaningful real-world situations, they tend to assess knowledge and skills in isolation and out of context. Selected-response items cannot fully measure certain valued learning outcomes, such as argumentation, oral communication, and social skills. Although real-world issues and problems rarely have single correct answers, the widespread use of assessments with selected-response formats may communicate to students an unintended message about the nature of knowledge and learning. They communicate that recognizing the "right answer" is the primary goal of education. Critics also express concerns that multiple-choice tests lead to "multiple-choice" teaching, that is, a focus on acquisition of facts rather than an emphasis on understanding and the thoughtful application of knowledge (Darling-Hammond & Adamson, 2013; Wiggins, 1992). With a recognition of their advantages and limitations, teachers may appropriately incorporate selected-response formats as part of a balanced menu of assessment methods.

Figure 3.1. Framework of Assessment Methods

	How might we assess student learning?			
	What methods are most appropriate given the learning goals and the purposes and audiences for the assessment?			
	Selected-Response Items	Brief Constructed Responses	Performance-Based Assessments		Process-Focused Assessments
			Products	*Performances*	
Example	❏ multiple-choice ❏ true-false ❏ matching ❏ technology-enhanced item; e.g., rank order several elements	❏ fill-in-the-blank ❏ word(s) ❏ phrase(s) ❏ short answer ❏ paragraph ❏ label a diagram ❏ Tweet ❏ "show your work" ❏ representation(s) *e.g., fill in a:* ❏ flow chart ❏ concept map ❏ label a diagram ❏ technology-enhanced item; *e.g., populate a data table*	❏ essay ❏ research paper blog/ journal lab report ❏ story/play ❏ infographic ❏ poem ❏ portfolio ❏ art exhibit ❏ science project model ❏ iMovie ❏ podcast	❏ oral presentation ❏ dance/movement ❏ science lab demonstration ❏ athletic skills performance ❏ dramatic reading ❏ TED Talk ❏ debate ❏ musical recital ❏ PowerPoint ❏ musical recital	❏ oral questioning ❏ observation ("kid watching") ❏ interview ❏ conference ❏ process description ❏ "think aloud" ❏ learning log ❏ interactive notebook ❏ student self-assessment

Figure 3.2. Classroom Examples of Selected-Response Items Assessment

Purpose: *diagnostic*

Prior to introducing photosynthesis, a high school biology teacher gives her students a multiple-choice pretest to assess their prior knowledge about the topic and check for any potential misconceptions—for example, Water is a source of food for plants. Using her department's scanning machine, she quickly determines that most students have limited knowledge about photosynthesis, while some harbor misconceptions. This information helps her plan instruction accordingly.

Assessment Purpose: *evaluative*

A college economics professor includes a multiple-choice section on his midterm and final examinations to assess students' knowledge of key concepts and principles presented in the course textbook. The results are used in conjunction with other factors (responses to essay questions, research paper, and project) to derive the course grade.

Assessment Purpose: *formative*

Upper elementary students take a practice quiz in which they match states with their capital cities. They then exchange papers with a partner and check each other's responses by consulting a U.S. map. Incorrect matches are identified for later review with a "study buddy." This use of formative assessment reinforces the learning as students independently check to verify and correct the answers of their fellow students.

Assessment Purpose: *diagnostic*

At the beginning of a coronavirus awareness unit, a middle school health teacher gives his students a true-false quiz to determine their knowledge of basic facts about the disease. Using a scoring key, the teacher quickly realizes that the majority of students hold several common misconceptions regarding the spread of the virus. This information helps the teacher to address these misconceptions during the unit.

The development of fair and valid tests using selected-response items is a challenging and time-consuming process. Although a complete treatment of this topic is beyond the scope of this publication, several excellent resources are available to assist teachers in designing assessments using selected-response formats. For more information, see Brookhart and Nitko (2019), McMillan (2014), and Popham (2013).

BRIEF CONSTRUCTED RESPONSE ASSESSMENTS

The second column in Figure 3.1 refers to assessments that call on students to construct a short response to a question or prompt. Unlike selected-response items that present students with options from which to choose, constructed-response items expect students "do" something—that is, to generate brief responses to questions, problems, or prompts. Familiar examples include fill-in-the-blank, short written answer, and label a diagram.

Note: Categorically, the term *constructed response* could refer to *any* assessment in which students provide their own response beyond simply selecting from given alternatives. However, in this book, we propose a narrower definition for this category—that is, that assessments using this format result in a short response, distinguished from assessments that involve the creation of a more detailed products (e.g., an essay) or performance demonstrations (e.g., a science lab demonstration).

Although brief constructed-response (BCR) items may seek a correct or acceptable response (e.g., fill-in-the-blank), they are more likely to yield a range of responses. Thus, the evaluation of student responses requires judgment, guided by criteria. This approach may be used for assessing declarative knowledge (factual knowledge) and procedural proficiency (skills). In addition, assessments using BCR items can provide insight into conceptual understanding (e.g., answer and explain items) and reasoning (e.g., items that require an argument supported by evidence or rationale) when students are requested to show their work and explain or defend their answers in writing.

Assessments using BCR items offer several advantages. They require less time to administer than more involved performance-based assessments. Since they elicit short responses, several BCR items may be used to assess learning of multiple content standards. However, BCR items are limited in their ability to adequately assess students' abilities to apply their learning in authentic contexts.

Some BCRs expect a "correct" answer, and these may be scored using an answer key. However, when a BCR is open-ended, teachers use judgment-based evaluation, which takes time and introduces potential problems of scoring reliability and fairness. Teachers are cautioned against regularly re-using brief constructed-response items for evaluative assessments so that students cannot give memorized responses to known or expected questions and tasks.

Figure 3.3 presents examples of classroom assessments using brief constructed-response formats for varied purposes and audiences.

Figure 3.3. Classroom Examples of Brief Constructed-Response Assessments

Assessment Purpose: *evaluative*

A middle school science teacher involves her students in an investigation of
the absorbency rates of different brands of paper towels. Following the
investigation, they plot the results of their data collection on a chart and
summarize their conclusions in writing. Students are evaluated on the
effectiveness with which their charts communicate the results and on the
accuracy of their written conclusions.

Assessment Purpose: *formative*

A middle school English teacher established a Twitter account for each class.
Students then create Tweets (up to 288 characters) in response to their
readings—for example, What is the major theme of the short story we read?
He reviews the Tweets to get a sense of the extent to which they are
comprehending various texts. The insights he gains helps him guide
subsequent class discussions.

Assessment Purpose: *evaluative*

As part of a unit test, a high school psychology teacher provides his students
with a comparison matrix containing different psychological theories on one
axis and various personality disorders on the other. They are asked to fill in
the cells of the matrix to explain the personality disorders according to each
theory.

Assessment Purpose: *formative*

A 6th-grade mathematics teacher asks her students to show their work as
they attempt to solve multistep word problems involving statistics and
probability. In addition to examining their solutions, she looks at their work
for evidence of appropriate use mathematical reasoning and problem-
solving strategies. She provides feedback through brief written comments.

PERFORMANCE-BASED ASSESSMENTS

Performance-based assessments include assessment activities that
result in students producing tangible products or performances to
serve as evidence of their learning. Well-designed performance assessments require students to "perform" with their learning—to apply knowledge and skills—rather than simply to recall and recognize.
Since performance-based assessments call for *application*, they are well
suited to assessing student understanding, integration of knowledge
across subject areas, and 21st-century skills such as effective decision

making, communication, and cooperation (Darling-Hammond & Adamson, 2013).

Performance-based assessments are sometimes referred to as *authentic assessments*, a term popularized by Grant Wiggins (Wiggins, 1989) to describe assessments that engage students in applying knowledge and skills in ways that they are used in the larger world beyond the school.

Performance-based assessments are generally open-ended, enabling a wide range of responses. Accordingly, evaluations of student products and performances are based on judgments guided by criteria that define the desired elements of quality (Ferrara et al., 1995). One widely used scoring tool is a *rubric*, which is used to evaluate the quality of products and performances. Rubrics consist of a fixed measurement scale (e.g., 4-point) and a list of criteria that describe the characteristics for each score point. (We will provide additional information and examples of rubrics in the next chapter.)

Authentic assessments typically present students with a genuine challenge, a target audience, and realistic constraints, and result in a tangible product or performance that serve as evidence of students' understanding and proficiency. Wiggins and McTighe (2012) offer the acronym GRASPS that can be used to develop an authentic context for an assessment task. The elements for each letter of the acronym for this practical and easy-to-remember design tool are summarized in Figure 3.4.

Figure 3.5 presents an example of a performance task used as part of an introductory unit on nutrition. Can you recognize the GRASPS elements contained within the task prompt?

Figure 3.4. GRASPS Framework

GRASPS

- A real-world **GOAL**,
- A meaningful **ROLE** for the student,
- An authentic (or simulated) **AUDIENCE**,
- A contextualized **SITUATION** that involves real-world application,
- Student-generated culminating **PRODUCT** and/or **PERFORMANCE**, and
- **SUCCESS** criteria by which student products and performances will be evaluated as evidence of learning.

Figure 3.5. Sample GRASPS Performance Assessment Task

Camp Menu

Since you have been learning about nutrition and healthy eating, you have been asked to plan a 3-day menu for meals and snacks for a camping trip over a holiday weekend. (Note: Refrigeration is available.) Develop your proposed menu, and explain why your menu plan is both "balanced" and tasty and should be adopted by the camping group.

You will notice that we have separated performance-based assessments into two types—products and performances (columns 4 and 5 on Figure 3.1) to illustrate various options. For example, students may produce written products (e.g., essays, research papers, laboratory reports, blog posts), visual products (e.g., two- and three-dimensional models, movies, infographics, murals), and aural products (e.g., a podcast). Figure 3.6 shows examples of product assessments.

One application of product assessment involves the systematic collection of representative samples of student work over time in portfolios (Niguidula, 2005, 2019). Portfolios enable teachers, students, parents, and others to observe performances or products at a point in time as well as to note growth in learning. Portfolio assessment has been widely used over the years in the visual arts, architecture, and technical areas and in some statewide alternate assessments of students with significant cognitive disabilities. More recently, teachers and schools involve students in assembling digital portfolios to document their learning in other subject areas, especially in English/language arts for writing.

As a companion to reviewing student products, teachers can directly observe actual performances by learners. Performances are naturally used to assess learning in certain subjects, including debate and discussion in literature and social studies, vocal and instrumental music, physical education, speech, theater, and dance where performance is the natural focus of instruction. Such performances are among the most authentic types of student assessments because they typically replicate the kinds of performances occurring in the world outside of school. However, teachers in other subjects can include performances, such as oral presentations, demonstrations, and debates, as part of an array of assessment methods. Many teachers and parents have observed that students are often motivated to put forth greater effort when they perform before "real" audiences of other students,

Figure 3.6. Classroom Examples of Product Assessments

Assessment Purpose: *evaluative*

Students develop a computer program for a high school coding class. Their teacher evaluates students' programming knowledge and skills by examining the program's written code for accuracy and efficiency. In addition, students must run the program to demonstrate that it performs the specified functions and produces specified results. Unsuccessful programs must be "debugged" until they satisfactorily fulfill the requirements.

Assessment Purpose: *formative*

A 4th-grade teacher collects biweekly examples of representative written work for each student in a language arts portfolio. The collected student samples are reviewed with parents during midyear conferences. The portfolio provides parents with tangible illustrations of their child's literacy development. The teacher uses the actual products, along with a developmental scale of reading and writing, to discuss the students' skill strengths and points out areas needing special attention.

Assessment Purpose: *evaluative*

A college engineering professor assigns his students to work in teams to design and build a self-propelled hovering vehicle that corresponds to certain specified parameters. In addition to the model, students must individually prepare a technical report related to their design. The models and technical reports are evaluated to determine students' understanding of, and ability to apply, principles of aerodynamics. A culminating "hovering" contest is used to determine the most effective designs.

Assessment Purpose: *evaluative* and *formative*

Middle school art students create a landscape using tempera paints. Using a skills checklist, their art teacher assesses their paintings to determine their proficiency in using the medium. He also assesses their understanding of the use of compositional elements for creating an illusion of depth. Individual student conferences are arranged to provide feedback.

Assessment Purpose: *formative*

A middle school science teacher reviews her students' laboratory reports to determine their effectiveness in applying experimental procedures and the accuracy of their data collection. Her written comments in the margins point out errors and offer specific suggestions for improvement. The reports are returned, discussed, and filed in the students' science folders for future reference.

staff, parents, or expert judges. Schools also benefit from positive public relations when students perform for the community. Figure 3.7 shows examples of performances that can be assessed.

Using products and performances to gather evidence of learning and proficiency has significant benefits. When students are given opportunities to produce authentic products and engage in actual performance, they often become more engaged in, and committed to, their learning because of the relevance of the context and their

Figure 3.7. Classroom Examples of Performances

Assessment Purpose: *formative*

Students in the school orchestra participate in a dress rehearsal 2 weeks before the public performance. The instrumental music teacher works with the students to evaluate their performance during the rehearsal and identify areas of weakness. During the ensuing practices, the orchestra members concentrate on making improvements in these areas prior to the actual performance before a live audience.

Assessment Purpose: *evaluative*

A high school social studies teacher sets up an in-class debate as a culminating activity for a unit on contemporary issues. Students work as part of a team to debate the issue of gun control. The teacher evaluates students' debate performances using a multitrait rubric including their understanding of the Bill of Rights and the Second Amendment, persuasiveness of their arguments, use of supporting evidence, effectiveness in countering rebuttals, and observance of rules of debating.

Assessment Purposes: *formative* **and** *evaluative*

An elementary physical education teacher uses a skills checklist during the unit on introductory gymnastics to assess students' proficiency. Each student receives a copy of the checklist and works with a partner to try to successfully perform the identified skills. The completed checklists are used as one component of the culminating grade for the unit.

Assessment Purpose: *evaluative*

A high school speech teacher works with a home economics teacher in preparing students to make oral presentations to communicate the results of a nutrition research project. The home economics teacher evaluates the students on accuracy and completeness of their knowledge of the USDA "food plate," while the speech teacher evaluates the oral presentations using a scoring rubric for an expository speech.

active involvement. Unlike statewide assessments that require uniform student responses, performance-based assessments are typically more open-ended, often allowing students some "voice and choice" through which to express their individuality. Moreover, since these types of assessments reflect real-world applications, they often involve interdisciplinary applications and the use of 21st-century skills, such as design thinking, collaboration, and multimedia communications.

Despite their benefits, performance-based assessments have their drawbacks. The time required for students to develop quality products and prepare for performances may compete with other instructional priorities. Sometimes students get sidetracked by working on "surface features" (e.g., decorating a science fair display board) at the expense of focusing on the essential content being assessed (scientific experimentation). Some product assessments require specific resources, including funds for materials and space for display and storage.

Since performance-based assessments rarely have a single correct answer, criteria for judging students' products and performances must be identified and used for evaluation, and this can be a time-consuming process. In addition, teachers must be careful when evaluating student work that their judgments are not unduly influenced by extraneous variables, such as neatness, spelling, or a student's behavior or prior performance.

PROCESS-FOCUSED ASSESSMENTS

Process-focused assessments provide information on students' learning strategies and thinking processes. Rather than focusing on tangible products or performances, this approach focuses on gaining insights into the underlying cognitive processes used by students. Teachers routinely use a variety of process-focused assessments as a natural part of teaching. For example, teachers may elicit students' thinking processes using oral questions such as: "How are these two things alike and different?" or by asking students to "think out loud" as they solve a problem or make a decision. Teachers may ask students to document their thinking over time by keeping a learning log. Also, teachers can learn about students' thinking processes by observing students as they function in the classroom. This "kid watching" method is especially well suited to assessing the development of attitudes or dispositions, such as persistence.

Figure 3.8. Classroom Examples of Process-Focused Assessments

Assessment Purpose: *formative*

A high school world history teacher has students keep an interactive notebook to add their own summaries and commentaries to his lectures, textbook readings, and primary source research they conduct. Each week he randomly selects several students' notebooks to review. Their entries give him valuable insights into how learners are making sense of the course content.

Assessment Purpose: *diagnostic*

A kindergarten teacher interviews each of her children in the beginning of the year. This informal assessment provides useful information about cognitive and linguistic development, social skills, and areas of personal interest.

Assessment Purpose: *formative*

A middle school teacher using project-based learning (PBL) uses a criterion checklist to regularly assess students' cooperative skills as they work in collaborative groups. Periodically, she selects students to serve as process observers, giving them the checklist of observable indicators of cooperative skills. Each week, the teacher and student observers provide descriptive feedback to the class on the effectiveness of their group processes, and students use the same checklist to self-assess their own performance in their group.

Assessment Purpose: *formative*

A high school mathematics teacher asks students to describe their reasoning processes by thinking out loud during the solution of open-ended problems. By listening to students as they articulate their thoughts, the teacher can identify fallacious reasoning and give feedback on the appropriateness of strategies they are using, thus providing needed assistance.

Process-focused assessments are formative in nature in that they provide *information* to teachers and feedback to students. They may be used to support the development of students' metacognition by heightening their awareness of their own cognitive processes and worthwhile strategies. Process-focused assessment methods are typically used over time, rather than on single occasions. To invoke the photographic analogy once again, think of process-focused assessments as a video camera that is always running, rather a moment in time "picture" offered by a test or task. Since their intent is to gather ongoing information as feedback for teachers and learners, we strongly discourage their use for evaluation and grading purposes. Figure 3.8 provides examples of process-focused assessments. As these examples suggest, process-focused assessments are most appropriately used for diagnostic and formative purposes.

CONCLUSION

In this chapter we have explored a variety of methods by which teachers can collect evidence of learning in their classrooms. The choice of methods depends on the targeted learning goal, the purposes for the assessment, and how the resulting information will be used. In the next chapter we will examine various methods for evaluating student performance and communicating the results.

Reflection Questions

- What classroom assessment methods do you currently employ?
- Are you using assessments to check students' prior knowledge (preassessments), for ongoing feedback (formative assessments), as well as to evaluate learning (evaluative assessments)?
- Are any important learning goals "falling through the cracks" because they are not being assessed properly—or at all?

CHAPTER 4

Evaluating Student Performance

Educational assessments are meant to elicit evidence of students' knowledge, skill level, conceptual understanding, and ability to apply (transfer) their learning. Once students have responded, the next phase of the assessment process involves evaluating the resulting responses, products and/or performances, and making use of the information gleaned. The third page of our assessment-planning framework addresses both evaluation and communication (Figure 4.1). In this chapter we will explore options for evaluating student responses, products, and performances to classroom assessments. The next chapter will examine various ways of communicating the results, including providing feedback on formative assessments and grading evaluative assessments.

The first column in Figure 4.1 displays an array of evaluation options, which we describe below.

Selected-response format items and some brief constructed-response items (e.g., fill-in-the-blank) yield a single correct or best answer. Most often teachers score such items using an answer key. Sometimes they ask students to "bubble in" their answers on an answer sheet that can be scanned by machine or hand-scored by overlaying a scoring template. Scoring of selected-response format items is relatively quick, easy, and objective, in large part because it yields a binary choice; that is, students' responses are either right or wrong!

In contrast, assessments that are open-ended (brief constructed response and performance based) elicit a range of responses, products, or performances that reflect varying degrees of conceptual understanding, proficiency, or quality. Because such assessments typically do not have a *single* correct answer, teachers must rely on judgment-based methods, based on clear and appropriate criteria, to evaluate responses to them. *Criterion lists* and *rubrics* are the most common types of evaluation tools used for evaluating students' responses and work on open-ended classroom assessments.

Figure 4.1. Evaluation and Communication Methods

Evaluation and Communication Methods

Evaluation Methods	Evaluation Roles	Communication/ Feedback Methods
How will we evaluate student knowledge and proficiency?	*Who will be involved in evaluating student responses, products or performances?*	*How will we communicate assessment results?*

Selected-Response Items:
 	
❑ answer key
❑ scoring template
❑ machine scoring
 	
<u>**Open-Ended Assessments:**</u>
 	
❑ criterion list
❑ scoring rubric
  • holistic
  • analytic
  • developmental
    continuum
	Judgment-Based Evaluation by:
	
	❑ teacher(s)/instructor(s)
	
	❑ peers
	
	❑ expert judges/external raters
	
	❑ student (self-evaluation)
	
	❑ parents/community members
	
	❑ others: _____
	(e.g. rating by viewers on the web)
		❑ numerical scores
		  * percentage scores
		  * point totals
		❑ letter grades
		
		❑ proficiency scale
		  * generic rubric
		  * task-specific rubric
		
		❑ developmental continuum
		❑ narrative report (written)
		❑ checklist
		❑ written comments
		❑ verbal report/conference

CRITERION LISTS

A straightforward and practical tool for evaluating student performance is simply a list of criteria or key elements and a scale. The scale can be quite flexible, ranging from as few as 3 points to 100%. Figure 4.2 shows an example of a criterion list for composing a modern-day fairy tale.

Figure 4.2. A Criterion List for a Modern-Day Fairy Tale

Trait	Criterion	Points	Weighting (Optional)	Student's Self-Assessment	Teacher's Evaluation
Fairy tale elements	Contains the elements of a fairy tale: an enchanted setting, magical elements, good and evil characters.				
Plot	The plot has a clear beginning, middle, and end.				
Details	The story contains descriptive details to describe the plot, setting, and characters.				
Pictures	Pictures are attractive and help to tell the story.				
Mechanics	Correct use of grammar, spelling, capitalization, and punctuation.				
	TOTALS				

Notice that this format enables teachers to score the various traits by assigning points to each of the respective criteria. When appropriate, this format enables a "weighting" of certain elements over others based on their relative importance based on the targeted learning goals. For example, the inclusion of all fairy tale elements would count for more than the pictures since this is a task that assesses an understanding of the characteristics of fairy tales rather than art skills. Also, the lists may be configured so as to easily convert to conventional letter grades, if need be. For example, a teacher could assign point values and weights that add up to 25, 50, or 100 points, enabling a straightforward conversion to a district or school grading scale (e.g., A = 90–100; B = 80–89; and so on). When the lists are shared with students in advance, they specify the "success criteria" to help learners understand how their work will be judged and which traits are most important. The format of these lists also encourages self-assessment and refinement by students as they work.

Wiggins and McTighe (2012) identify four general categories of criteria—content, process, quality, and impact. Here are descriptions of each type with an illustrative example:

1. *Content* criteria are used to evaluate the degree of a student's knowledge and understanding of facts, concepts, and principles specified in a content standard. *Was the explanation of the historical event accurate and complete?*
2. *Process* criteria are used to evaluate the effectiveness of the methods and procedures used in a task, as well as the proficiency level of a skill performance specified in process (practices) standards. *How well did the student follow the protocol for conducting the survey?*
3. *Quality* criteria are used to evaluate the overall quality and craftsmanship of a product or performance. *What is quality of the art student's use of tempora paints?*
4. *Impact* criteria are used to evaluate the overall results, given the purpose and audience. *Did the debate performance convince the judges?*

Note that the type of criteria selected should be directly aligned to the learning goal(s) being evaluated. In some cases, a single criterion type is all that is needed, whereas a complex performance, reflecting several goals, may require more than one. For example, a persuasive essay could be judged against *content, quality,* and *impact* criteria.

Figure 4.3. A Single-Point Rubric for Formative Assessment of a Data Display

Needs Work	Criteria	Strong Work
	1. The graph contains a title that tells what the data show.	
	2. All parts of the graph (units of measurement, rows, etc.) are correctly labeled.	
	3. All data are accurately represented on the graph.	
	4. The graph is neat and easy to read.	

A variation on a criterion list is sometimes called a *single-point rubric* (Gonzales, 2015). Although technically this tool is not a rubric since it does not contain descriptions of graduated performance levels on a scale, it nonetheless can be a valuable tool for formative assessment and feedback. A single-point rubric consists of three columns with the key performance traits listed in the center. The left column is blank, enabling the teacher (or a peer) to provide feedback on weaknesses and target areas needing improvement. The right column is also blank to enable the teacher (or peer) to highlight strengths. Figure 4.3 shows an example of a single-point rubric for a data display.

Note that the single-point rubric does not have a place for scores or ratings. It is intended as a feedback tool for use in formative assessment rather than a tool for evaluation and grading.

To be most effective for its purpose, teachers (or peers) need to provide written feedback or schedule a one-to-one conversation with the student.

Despite their practical qualities, criterion lists and single-point rubrics have limits. Most notably, they do not provide detailed descriptions of various performance levels. In other words, there are no qualitative descriptions of the difference between an "8" and a "15" rating for a given trait. Thus, despite identified criteria, different teachers using the same performance list may rate the same student's work differently. Similarly, students may not understand what they need to do to improve simply by seeing the summary rating or score on the list.

RUBRICS

Like a criterion list, a rubric consists of evaluative criteria. However, rubrics add a fixed performance scale (e.g., 4 or 6 points) and, most

significantly, a description of the levels of performance at each scale
point or level to discriminate among different degrees of understanding, proficiency, or quality. Sometimes, rubrics are supported by student work or performances that exemplify each score point (i.e.,
anchors; see discussion below).

The term has its origins in the Latin word *rubrica*, meaning "red
earth" used to mark something of significance. In a similar vein, educators today use rubrics to communicate the important qualities in a
product or performance and guide their evaluations of students' work.
There are three basic types of rubrics used in educational assessments:
holistic, analytic, and developmental.

Holistic Rubrics

A holistic rubric provides an overall impression of a student's performance, yielding a single rating or score. The rubric in Figure 4.4 presents
an example of a holistic rubric for evaluating reading comprehension.

Holistic rubrics can be used to gauge the overall quality or impact of a student's work—for example, To what extent was the essay
persuasive? Did the experiment confirm or disprove the hypothesis?

Figure 4.4. A Holistic Rubric for Reading

Scale	Evaluative Criteria
4	Reader displays a sophisticated understanding of the text with substantial evidence of comprehension of ideas stated explicitly and inferentially. Multiple connections are made between the text and the reader's ideas/experiences. Interpretations are sophisticated and directly supported by appropriate text references. Reader explicitly takes a critical stance—for example, analyzes the author's style, questions the text, provides alternative interpretations, views the text from multiple perspectives.
3	Reader displays a solid understanding of the text with clear evidence of comprehension of ideas stated explicitly and inferentially. Connections are made between the text and the reader's ideas/experiences. Interpretations are made and generally supported by appropriate text references. Reader may reveal a critical stance toward the text.
2	Reader displays a superficial understanding with limited comprehension of ideas in the text. No connections are made between the text and the reader's ideas/experiences. Reader provides no interpretations or evidence of a critical stance.
1	Reader displays minimal or no evidence of text comprehension.

Did the story entertain the readers? Since they offer an overall rating, holistic rubrics are well suited to assigning a grade for an assignment or performance task. However, they are less effective on their own at providing precise feedback to learners about what they have done well and the particular areas needing improvement. In other words, holistic rubrics can serve as effective tools for evaluating a student's work but provide little guidance as to how they could improve it.

Holistic rubrics can also present a challenge for teachers when they are used to evaluate a complex performance having multiple dimensions. For example, consider two different students who have completed a graphic design project: One student uses visual symbols to clearly communicate an abstract idea. However, her design involves clip art images that are sloppily pasted onto the graphic. A second student creates a beautiful and technically sophisticated design, yet his main idea is trivial. How would those respective pieces be scored using a holistic rubric? Often, the compromise involves "averaging," whereby both students might receive the same score or grade, yet for substantially different reasons. Without more detailed feedback than a score or rating, it is difficult for the student to know exactly what the grade means or what refinements are needed in the future. These problems can be addressed through the use of an analytic (or multi-trait) rubric described below.

Analytic Rubrics

An analytic rubric also contains a performance scale but divides a targeted product or performance into distinct elements or traits and judges each independently. Figure 4.5 presents an example for an oral presentation.

Analytic rubrics are well suited to judging students' work on performance-based assessments involving several significant dimensions. Notice in the example above that the rubric identifies four important traits of an effective oral presentation (*content, organization, delivery,* and *language conventions*), and each trait is evaluated on its own 4-point scale. Thus, analytic rubrics provide more specific information (feedback) to students, parents, and teachers about the strengths and weaknesses of a performance.

Although holistic rubrics have their place, holistic ratings (on their own) provide little meaningful guidance about how to do a better job in the future. How can students improve their research skills, for instance, if all they receive is a "3" (or a "B–") on a holistic rubric

Figure 4.5. An Analytic Rubric for Oral Presentations

Scale	Content	Organization	Delivery	Conventions
4	Extremely clear, accurate, and complete	Coherent organization throughout; logical sequence; smooth transitions; effective introduction and conclusion	Fluid, polished delivery; excellent and appropriate volume with varied intonation; effective body language and eye contact enhance the message	Highly effective use of language enhances the message; grammatically correct
3	Generally clear, accurate, and complete	Good organization overall, but with occasional breaks in the logical flow of ideas; clear transitions; identifiable introduction and conclusion	Effective delivery; adequate volume and intonation; body language and eye contact support the message	Generally effective use of language supports the message; minor grammatical errors do not detract from the message
2	Parts of the content are unclear, inaccurate, and/or incomplete	Flawed organization; ideas not well developed; weak transitions; ineffective opening and/or conclusion	Delivery is uneven; volume is too low or too loud; monotone delivery; body language and eye contact do not enhance the message	Use of language is not always aligned with the message; grammatical errors may detract from the message
1	Overall, the content is unclear, inaccurate, and incomplete	Lack of organization; difficult to follow the flow of ideas; weak transitions; no introduction or conclusion	Message cannot be understood due to low volume and strained delivery; speaker fails to make eye contact; posture is poor	Numerous errors in language conventions make the message difficult to follow

for their research report? Accordingly, we recommend that teachers use analytic rubrics for day-to-day, formative assessments in their classrooms. Since they identify and evaluate particular traits, analytic rubrics provide more detailed and targeted feedback to students about the strengths of their performance and the areas needing attention. If the goal is to improve student learning, not simply grade it, then such specific feedback is needed. For example, a student receiving the following descriptive comments on an analytic rubric—"uses several appropriate sources to gather information on the topic" and "needs to document all sources using standard bibliographic notation"—is informed both about a strength of the research (use of multiple sources) and a weakness (lack of complete documentation). Now the student knows what to attend to the next time she works on a research paper.

Since there are several traits to be considered, the use of an analytic scoring rubric may take a bit more time than assigning a single score. However, for use in classroom assessments, we believe that the more specific feedback that results is well worth the effort, especially given the ultimate goal of improving learning and performance.

Fortunately, the choice between these two types of rubrics does not require an either/or decision. Indeed, teachers can use both during a course or unit of study—for example, use analytic rubric "along the way" as part of formative assessments to inform teaching and guide student practice and revision. Then, they can employ holistic rubric(s) at the conclusion of a performance task or unit assessment to provide an overall evaluation of, and grade for, student performance.

Generic and Task-Specific Rubrics

In addition to analytic or holistic types, a rubric may also be *generic* or *task specific*. A generic rubric provides general criteria for evaluating a student's performance in a given performance area. The rubrics shown in Figures 4.4 and 4.5 are examples of generic rubrics since they may be used to evaluate a variety of reading tasks and oral presentations, respectively.

In contrast, a task-specific rubric is designed for use with a *particular* assessment task. For example, the art rubric in Figure 4.6 is used to assess the task of comparing the styles and techniques of two artists (Matisse and van Allsburg) and indicating a preference. Notice that a task-specific rubric, such as this one, cannot be used to evaluate responses to different performance tasks since at least some of its wording is unique to a very specific task or assignment.

Generic rubrics have the advantage of being applicable to multiple assessment activities within a subject area, such as expository writing, mathematical problem solving, and research. Rather than creating a

Figure 4.6. A Task-Specific Rubric for Visual Art

Scale	Evaluative Criteria
3	• Identifies three or more relevant differences between the work of Matisse and van Allsburg (e.g., use of color, level of detail/simplification, use of line and shape, materials, process). • Identifies a preference for one artist's style. • Supports their preference with two or more well-stated reasons citing specific examples from the artist's work. • Uses a variety of art vocabulary terms appropriately.
2	• Identifies two relevant differences between the work of Matisse and van Allsburg. • Identifies a preference for one artist's style. • Supports their preference with one reason citing an example from the artist's work. • Uses one or two art vocabulary terms appropriately.
1	• Does not clearly identify significant differences between the work of Matisse and van Allsburg. • Identifies a preference for one artist's style but does not support their preference with reasons or examples. • Does not use art vocabulary terms appropriately.

new rubric for each and every performance task, the same rubric can be taught to students, posted in the room, and used throughout the year (and often across grade levels). With repeated use, the criteria contained in the generic rubric can be internalized by students so that they are better able to consider the qualities of effective performance *while* they are working, as well as to evaluate their own work when they are finished.

Despite the benefits of generic rubrics, there are times when a task-specific rubric will be preferable. Task-specific rubrics tend to yield greater reliability (consistency of evaluation) when used by different teachers. Thus, a department or grade-level team might employ a task-specific rubric for use with a common performance task or final exam given by more than one teacher. The good news is that task-specific rubrics can be derived, and customized, from generic rubrics.

Developmental Rubrics

A third type of rubric—developmental—describes growth along a proficiency continuum, ranging from novice to expert. The colored belts that designate various proficiency levels in karate or the developmental rubric for swimming from the Red Cross are examples. Longitudinal versions of developmental rubrics are well suited to subjects that emphasize skill performance. Hence, they are natural to English language arts, physical education, the arts, and language acquisition. The American Council on the Teaching of Foreign Languages (ACTFL) has developed sets of longitudinal proficiency rubrics that are widely used for profiling performance levels for speaking, listening, and reading in world languages. (See http://oflaslo.weebly.com/proficiency-rubrics .html#.X6nyzFfPxXs.)

Developmental (also known as *longitudinal* or *competency*) rubrics are generic in that they are not tied to any particular performance task or even age/grade levels. Thus, teachers across the grades can profile student proficiency levels on the same rubric. Furthermore, an agreed-on developmental scale enables learners, teachers, and parents to collectively chart *progress* over time as well as moment-in-time performances.

Perhaps the greatest advantage of well-designed rubrics of all types is their clear delineation of the elements of success or quality. They provide teachers with specific criteria for reliably evaluating student responses, products, or performances; a tool for increasing the consistency of evaluation among teachers; and clear targets for instruction. They provide students with the success criteria that serve as learning/ performance targets, expectations about what is most important, and criteria for self-evaluation and self-improvement.

A common concern about the use of rubrics when evaluating student work on open-ended, performance assessments is that the scoring is too subjective. Although we agree that this can be a potential problem—especially with poorly designed tasks and scoring rubrics— we do not agree that the challenge is insurmountable. After all, we use judgment-based evaluations routinely in state writing assessments, AP art portfolio reviews, in Olympic events, and when we rate a restaurant. Indeed, there are well-established practices that enable performance assessments and judgment-based evaluation to function fairly, consistently, and defensibly (Arter & McTighe, 2001; Gareis & Grant, 2015). Here is a summary of actions to make it more likely that performance assessments and associated rubrics will yield valid and reliable measures:

1. Develop clear assessment prompts, directions, and parameters for the performance assessment task.
2. Ensure that the task will elicit students' responses directly aligned to the targeted learning goal(s).

3. Identify clear and specific criteria for evaluating student performance and embed these in an evaluation tool (e.g., a rubric). Identify the traits that characterize the most salient attributes of successful application and operationally define these. Be careful not to focus only on the surface features of a product or performance (e.g., neatness, mechanics, unless those are part of the intended learning!).

4. When common performance tasks are used across classrooms, we recommend the use of agreed-on rubrics to promote more consistent evaluation of student performance by teachers.

5. Whenever possible, work with a team to jointly score student work using interrater reliability procedures to increase consistency of judgments (i.e., two to four teachers score the same work independently, then compare and discuss their ratings). Professional learning communities (PLCs) offer a perfect structure for this process.

6. Over time, collect samples of student work (anchors) that illustrate the different performance levels in a rubric, and annotate the samples (i.e., describe in writing why a piece of work was scored as it was). These samples can then be shared with your students as part of the teaching–learning process. Sharing samples may prove to be especially important in online environments where they can't be posted in a physical space.

Although we recognize that it will not be feasible to go into such detail with every single performance assessment or rubric used by individual teachers, we strongly recommend that such a process be used for important common assessments and recurring tasks—for example, for writing (expository, narrative, persuasive), mathematical reasoning and problem solving, scientific investigation, historical research, and artistic production.

EVALUATION ROLES

In most classrooms, the teacher is the primary evaluator. However, others can play a role in evaluating student achievement, especially on performance-based assessments and in conjunction with project-based learning. Indeed, teachers may involve other staff members, parents, or community experts in the evaluation of student products (e.g., science fair projects) and performances (e.g., public speaking exhibitions).

Many schools have established PLC structures, which are well suited for the valuable process of teachers working in teams to evaluate student work on common performance-based assessments using common rubrics. Teachers who have experienced such group scoring of evaluative assessments often comment on the significant professional benefits they derive by working with colleagues in this way. (We discuss the use of PLCs again in Chapter 7.)

Teachers may also involve students. We have observed that when students are engaged in applying criteria for peer *assessment*, they come to understand and internalize the elements of quality and performance standards in ways that can lead to improvements in the quality of their *own* work. Note that we used the phrase *peer assessment* rather than *peer evaluation*. Our advice is to use peer assessments primarily for "feedback" rather than for evaluation and grading. That is the teacher's job.

By regularly having students self-assess their work based on established criteria, teachers help learners to better understand the qualities that matter in their work and develop the capacity for honest self-appraisal, a quintessential characteristic of a self-directed learner.

The middle column of Figure 4.1 presents five possible evaluation roles beyond the classroom teacher. Here a few examples:

PLC Team Scoring

A team of three 5th-grade teachers meets each quarter on an early-release day to evaluate students' work on a common performance assessment. The work pieces from all three classes are mixed together, and the teachers use an agreed-on scoring rubric for the evaluation. Each piece of work is judged independently by two teachers, with the third weighing in when there are score discrepancies. This interrater reliability procedure helps to ensure that all teachers are applying the rubric consistently.

Project-Based Learning (PBL) Presentations Judged by Experts

Secondary school students work as a team to present the results of their multiweek project to a panel of adult experts. The experts use a 4-point rating sheet to evaluate the performance of each group on four traits: accuracy and depth of content, quality of the written summary, effectiveness of the multimedia presentation, and efficiency of problem solving. In addition to the expert judges, each student evaluates (1) their own performance in their group, and (2) the performance of the other group members, using a cooperation rubric.

Local Employers Review Students in a Mock Interview

High school juniors and seniors meet with a local employer for a mock interview either in person or using Zoom or Google chat or another video connection. In preparation, the students pick a business or governmental organization in their area. They conduct research to learn about various positions that interest them and develop a sample résumé to present to the employer. Students are judged by the employer during the interview based on the following traits: knowledge of the business and desired position(s), communication skills (including eye contact and body language), quality of questions, professional appearance, poise, and enthusiasm for position. Following the interview, students receive oral and written feedback along with their ratings on each trait.

Parents/Community Members Serve as Audience for TED Talks

During a week in the spring, all 8th-graders in the district present a 6-minute TED Talk on an approved topic of their choice, again either in person or online, to an audience of parents, community members, and school faculty. In preparation for their talk, students research their topic and prepare a written draft of the speech. They study award-winning TED Talks to learn about effective multimedia presentation techniques, and are given a rubric that they use to score other non-award-winning TED Talks and discuss needed improvements. They conduct practice sessions in front of peers who give them feedback using a criterion list. Community members rate each talk using the same list, and students receive the listeners' ratings, but the talks are not graded. The following week, teachers debrief the experience.

Teachers observe that their students generally put forth greater effort when they know that they and/or their work will be viewed by a genuine audience beyond the teacher. We encourage teachers to look for such opportunities for such authentic performances.

CONCLUSION

In this chapter we have explored a variety of methods by which teachers can evaluate student performance. In the next chapter, we will consider options for communicating these results based on various assessment purposes and audiences.

Reflection Questions

- What is your experience using rubrics to evaluate students' performances? Have you used both holistic and analytic rubrics? What successes and challenges have you experienced using rubrics?
- Do you have an existing assessment or assignment that you may want to adjust by incorporating the GRASPS elements?
- Do you present the "success criteria" (or associated scoring tool) to learners in advance of an open-ended assessment? If so, what effects have you observed?
- Do colleagues, parents, and/or students have concerns about potential subjectivity associated with evaluating open-ended assessments? If so, how might you alleviate their concerns?
- Do you engage your students in using established criterion lists and/or rubrics for self-assessment? If so, what are the effects?

CHAPTER 5

Communicating Assessment Results

You can assess students using various methods and evaluate their responses using appropriate scoring tools—but you're not done! It is now time to consider ways of communicating the assessment results. A variety of methods can be used to communicate assessment results, including numerical scores, letter grades, developmental scales, checklists, verbal and written comments/reports, and conferences. The choice of communication methods should be made according to the assessment purposes and formats, evaluation methods, feasibility considerations (e.g., time required), and especially the audience for the assessment. Fundamentally, the goal is to clearly and accurately communicate information (e.g., regarding achievement, progress, work habits) such that intended audiences (e.g., students, parents, teachers, receiving schools) will understand and can make proper use of that information. The third column of Figure 5.1 presents these various communication methods.

Before examining the features and limitations of specific communication methods, let us return to the three primary purposes of classroom and school-level assessments and their respective audiences.

Diagnostic assessments primarily serve educators. At the classroom level, they are conducted at the beginning point in an instructional cycle to determine students' proficiency levels, check for misconceptions, and reveal interests and experiences. Their results can inform instructional groupings and the need for differentiated instruction. At the school level, diagnostic assessments are regularly used for program placements—for example, preschool screenings used for youngsters entering pre-K or kindergarten to determine school readiness. A diagnostic mathematics assessment might be administered at the end of 8th grade, in conjunction with middle school grades, to target students eligible for Advanced Placement (AP) math courses in high school.

Figure 5.1. Evaluation and Communication Methods

Evaluation and Communication Methods

Evaluation Methods	Evaluation Roles	Communication/ Feedback Methods
How will we evaluate student knowledge and proficiency?	*Who will be involved in evaluating student responses, products or performances?*	*How will we communicate assessment results?*
Selected-Response Items:	**Judgment-Based Evaluation by:**	☐ numerical scores • percentage scores • point totals
☐ answer key ☐ scoring template ☐ machine scoring	☐ teacher(s)/instructor(s) ☐ peers	☐ letter grades
Open-Ended Assessment:	☐ expert judges/external raters	☐ proficiency scale • generic rubric • task-specific rubric
☐ criterion list ☐ scoring rubric • holistic • analytic • developmental continuum	☐ student (self-evaluation) ☐ parents/community members ☐ others: _____ (e.g. rating by viewers on the web)	☐ developmental continuum ☐ narrative report (written) ☐ checklist ☐ written comments ☐ verbal report/conference

© 2020 Jay McTighe and Steve Ferrara; adapted from McTighe and Ferrara (1997). *Assessing Learning in the Classroom*. Washington, DC: National Education Association.

Formative assessments are intended to advance learning by providing feedback on the teaching and learning process. For years, researchers have conclusively shown that the regular use of formative assessment and feedback in classrooms is one of the highest yielding educational interventions (Black & Wiliam, 1998; Hattie, 2012; Marzano, 2003). At its essence, formative assessment sets up a feedback loop whereby information on learning is "fed back" (i.e., communicated) to its primary audiences—teachers and students. In other words, the key to effective formative assessment is communication of information that can lead to improvement.

In contrast to diagnostic and formative assessments, the purpose of *evaluative assessments* is to the judge the amount or quality of learning. Summative evaluations and grades should be derived from the results of evaluative assessments designed to enable students to demonstrate accumulated proficiency related to identified content goals. The results of evaluative assessments are typically reported to students and parents, often as grades on classroom assessments and on report cards issued periodically (e.g., each quarter of the school year). These results, especially "marks" listed on report cards, are typically shared with administrators and become part of a student's permanent, cumulative record. This accumulative record, also known as a transcript, can be made available to the next school level, institutions of higher education, and employers.

To reiterate: What, and how, we communicate assessment results depends on what is being assessed, the purpose(s) of the assessment, and the audience(s) for that information. Next, we'll examine various communication methods.

COMMUNICATION METHODS

Numerical scores (e.g., percentage correct or number of points earned on a classroom quiz) and *letter grades* are widely used methods for communicating the results of classroom assessments. Both methods are efficient to use and succinct, but numerical scores and grades, by themselves, do not explicitly communicate the elements of quality and standards of performance that they are meant to reflect. For example, saying that 74% correct is a "C" can mean one thing on an easy task and something different on a difficult task. Moreover, the grade or number alone does not specify what a student knows, understands, and can do. Likewise, if students are graded "on a curve," their knowledge or performance level is judged and communicated simply in relation to other students in the class, not in terms of established criteria and standards.

Rubrics and developmental scales are generally more informative than numerical scores and grades because they contain descriptions of different degrees of knowledge and levels of proficiency. Information about student learning presented in terms of developmental levels can be especially meaningful to parents. Recognizing this fact, some districts and schools have revised their report cards accordingly, especially for the primary grades.

Checklists can also be effective for communicating assessment results because they present ratings-specific information about attained competencies. They are a quick and efficient method for providing direct and timely feedback to students. However, checklist developers must be careful to avoid categories, such as critical thinking or creativity, that may be difficult to define, do not generalize across domains, and can be open to diverse interpretations.

Written comments, narrative reports, verbal reports, and *conferences* can be effective communication methods because they provide opportunities to clearly and directly connect student effort and achievement to standards of performance. They also enable teachers to provide more personalized information than the other communication methods. Regrettably, the time-consuming nature of these methods often limits their use, especially for teachers at the secondary level serving high numbers of students.

Here are examples of various communications tools and methods in use.

Report Card: Personalized

A school district uses a reporting system that distinguishes student achievement of content standards from work habits and reports each separately. A unique feature of their system is its software database containing sets of preloaded narrative comments, organized by grade levels (pre-K–2, 3–5, 6–8, and 9–12) and associated with subject area standards and the district-identified list of work habits. When preparing report cards, teachers can then select appropriate comments for inclusion on the "narrative" section of the card. Figure 5.2 shows an illustrative sample for work habits. Note that the student's first name is included in the initial entry and the text appears handwritten to provide a more personalized look and feel.

Figure 5.2. A Personalized Report

Rating scale: 4 = always, 3 = usually, 2 = sometimes, 1 = rarely or never

Work Habits	Rating (1–4)	Comments
2. Completes class assignments and homework on time.	4	Roberta is a diligent student who always completes her work on time.
4. Participates in class.	3	She participates in class discussions when called on, but rarely volunteers. While participating, she does not take the lead in group activities.

Analytic Rubric

A middle school language arts teacher uses analytic rubrics for evaluating student performance and communicating with them. These rubrics include two simple graphic additions for encouraging student self-evaluation and goal setting. Figure 5.3 shows an example of a public speaking rubric. The first is the inclusion of two tiny check boxes at the bottom of each cell of an analytic rubric. The check boxes on the left can be used by students to self-assess their work before they turn it in to the teacher. The teacher then uses the other box for the "official" evaluation.

Once the assignment or task is scored and returned, students can compare the ratings. In cases when the two judgments do not match, teachers can use this as an opportunity to discuss the criteria, expectations, and performance standards. Over time, teacher and student judgments tend to align.

The second addition is the goals/action box located at the bottom of the rubric. Once their work is returned with feedback, students are expected to identify one or more goals for the future and/or actions that they will take to improve their performance. These simple additions can upgrade a rubric from being solely an evaluation instrument for scoring/grading to a practical tool for feedback, self-assessment, and goal setting.

Developmental Rubrics

All teachers of world languages in a district use the proficiency rubrics from the American Council on the Teaching of Foreign Languages

Figure 5.3. Analytic Rubric for Public Speaking

	Volume	Rate of Speech/Pacing	Eye Contact	Posture
4	Speaker projects with a strong, clear voice that can easily be heard by all.	Speech is delivered at a comfortable and appropriate pace.	Speaker establishes and maintains excellent eye contact throughout.	Speaker maintains excellent posture, displaying both confidence and composure.
3	Speaker speaks at a volume that can generally be heard without strain.	Speech is delivered at an appropriate pace, with occasional pauses.	Speaker makes eye contact with the audience but has occasional lapses.	Speaker maintains good posture and composure.
2	Speaker uses a soft voice that makes it difficult to hear the message.	Speech is too slow or too fast with frequent pauses.	Speaker makes intermittent eye contact with the audience.	Speaker displys poor posture and displays a lack of confidence.
1	Speaker speaks extremely softly and/or mumbles so that the message cannot be heard or understood.	Speech is halting and uneven with long pauses OR speech is delivered so rapidly that the audience is unable to follow or understand it.	Speaker makes little or no eye contact with audience.	Speaker slouches and fidgets, displaying extreme discomfort and lack of confidence.

Goals and Actions for Improvement:

(ACTFL) for evaluating and reporting performance levels for listening, speaking, reading, and writing. These developmental rubrics enable students (and parents) to see their current performance levels, while enabling them to track improvements over time. The ACTFL proficiency levels serve as the primary communication method used on the quarterly report cards, with traditional letter grades being reserved for work habits and reported separately.

Checklists

Secondary physical education teachers use a district-developed checklist of sports and fitness skills in rating their students. The checklists are loaded onto tablets so that that teachers can observe and rate students' proficiency levels (*beginner, developing, proficient, advanced*) over the course of a marking period and then print out final reports for each student. This approach aligns with the district's move to competency-based education and replaces the traditional letter grade previously used on report cards.

Oral Communications

An elementary school conducts student-involved conferences for parents. Students keep work folders for reading, writing, and mathematics that serve as a focal point for the conference. Students display selections of their work and explain to their parent(s) what they are learning. Teachers elaborate or explain as needed. Then, the teacher assists the student in targeting specific learning goals for the next few weeks. The teacher describes classroom activities that will occur and makes suggestions of ways that the parent(s) can support that learning at home.

Peer Feedback

Students in a 2-D studio art course meet in groups three times during the semester to conduct peer critique sessions on their developing artworks. Each group consist of 5–6 students who follow an established protocol to give each other feedback on the works based on established criteria. The art teacher has observed that students are particularly attentive to the feedback of their classmates and that the process contributes to the high-quality art that is produced and exhibited at the Board of Education office.

GRADING PRINCIPLES AND PRACTICES

Although we have presented a variety of options for communicating assessment results, the reality for most teachers is that their district or school uses a standardized reporting system of letter grades for communicating the results of evaluative assessments, especially on report cards. However, even when the reporting format is standardized, we have observed that the *determination* of grades can vary widely among teachers. For example, some teachers factor in class participation, homework completed on time, and attendance; others simply average quiz and test scores. Some teachers consider how much progress a student has made over the course of a marking period; others take off points for bad behavior. Some teachers allow students to earn extra credits while others do not. The point is clear—when different teachers consider different factors and weight them differently when computing report card grades, the meaning of grades as vehicles of communication is compromised.

Accordingly, we recommend that schools adopt a set of principles to undergird effective and consistent grading practices that will be most effective at communicating student learning. Here are four grading principles that reflect the recommendations of leading experts on the practices of grading and reporting (Brookhart et al., 2020; Guskey, 2020a; O'Connor, 2003).

Principle 1: The primary purpose of grades is to communicate
student achievement based on clearly articulated learning goals
and established criteria.

A grade should represent a definable degree of achievement related to targeted outcomes.

Accordingly, educators need to be able to clearly describe each goal, describe the criteria and performance standards by which they will measure success, assess students accordingly, and (finally) report the results in a clear and consistent manner. These are the essential steps of *standards-based grading*, which is criterion referenced.

Criterion-referenced grading differs from norm-referenced evaluation and grading, whereby a student's grade is determined by how well that student compares to others in the class. (The now discredited practice of "grading in a curve" is an example.) In a norm-referenced system, a student might earn an "A" for being the "best" performer in a class of very low achievers or a "C–" for being a "below average" student in a class of advanced learners. Further, norm-based grading can promote unhealthy competition in which some students will necessarily become "winners" and others "losers" as they compete for scarce rewards—that is, a limited number of A's and B's.

Note: In those cases where a student is working on an Individualized Education Program (or Plan; IEP) because of special needs or when they are placed in an accelerated program, then appropriate assessment measures need to be identified for their *personalized* goals, and those results will provide the basis for their grading.

Principle 2: Grades should be based on evidence derived from sound assessment of targeted goals.

As discussed, an assessment is sound if it enables valid inferences about desired results—that is, if it measures what we intend it to measure and not extraneous factors. Poorly crafted or misaligned assessments will result in nonrepresentative and misleading communications about a student's achievement. In other words, the grades are only as good as the associated assessment measures.

Moreover, assessment purpose must be taken into account—not all assessment results should be factored into grades. For example, diagnostic assessments are not evaluative, and thus their results should not be factored into achievement grades. It would be unfair to hold learners accountable for what they knew (or didn't know) before instruction. Similarly, formative assessments should rarely be factored into a final grade since these assessments are meant to provide feedback to teachers and students for improvement. Evaluative assessments, administered after a specified period of instruction, are the ones that serve to enable teachers to judge what students know, understand, and can do. The evidence from these assessments becomes the basis for grades.

Principle 3: Separate the grading and reporting of achievement from other factors.

It is often the case that grades for a marking period reflect a mixture of multiple factors. For instance, it is possible that three students in the same class could earn the same grade (e.g., a "B") for very different reasons: One is a very able student who knows the material at an "A" level but does not complete assignments; the second is a solid "B" student; the third has significant learning challenges but works very hard and has shown significant improvement during the marking period, even though she has not mastered some key skills in the standards. This example makes the point: When other ingredients beyond achievement are factored into a grade (e.g., effort, completing work on time, class participation, progress, attendance, homework, attitude, behavior), the meaning of that grade becomes fuzzy. This problem transcends individual teachers. Unless teachers throughout a school or district completely agree on the elements and factor them into their grading in consistent ways, the meaning of grades will vary from classroom to classroom, school to school.

As a practical approach to acting on our principle 3, assessment and grading authority Tom Guskey (2020b) makes the case against relying on a single report grade for communication and recommends a 3Ps approach to grading and reporting. We strongly endorse his idea. Here it is: The first P refers to *performance* (or academic achievement). As noted in principles 1 and 2, students would be evaluated on their performance related to specific learning goals based on the results of appropriate assessments and performance standards. A performance grade for a subject, or for specific standards within, would be reported on the report card. A separate grade would be assigned for a second P, *process*. Process factors refer to elements that are considered important to learning and would be identified and operationally defined by the district or school. Process factors might include elements such as work habits, class participation, homework, social and emotional learning (SEL) competencies, and collaboration with peers. Reporting process factors separately acknowledges their value without integrating them into the achievement grade, which muddies the communications' waters. The third P refers to *progress*, defined as growth or improvement from a designated starting place to a student's current level of achievement. By evaluating, gauging, and reporting on progress, educators can honor students' developmental progress and support a growth mindset in students. Progress marking is especially natural when districts, schools, or programs use developmental rubrics, such as the ACTFL rubrics for world languages.

The key point in Guskey's triad is that these three factors—performance, process, and progress—are treated as independent variables that will be evaluated and reported separately. Using a 3Ps approach will make grades and associated reports clearer, more honest, and more effective vehicles for communication.

Principle 4: Let performance grades reflect current achievement.

Grades should be based on a synthesis of evidence reflecting students' current level of learning or accomplishment. Note that this principle contradicts the widespread practice of averaging scores over the course of a marking period to arrive at a numerically based final grade. Tomlinson and McTighe (2006) offer a humorous anecdote to illustrate the problem of averaging scores in this way: "A man is sitting on an old-fashioned room radiator that is blisteringly hot. His bare feet rest on a block of frigid ice. When asked about the room temperature, he replies, 'On average, it's pretty comfortable!' This humorous story has a serious point—averages can mislead" (p. 132).

Grades reflects an end-point judgment about student achievement. If our goal is to document learning, it should not matter where students were at the beginning of a marking period or even halfway through a learning sequence. What matters is what they have learned and are able to do at the end. As an alternative to averaging all the marks from start to finish, we join other grading experts who recommend that teachers evaluate students' achievements *later* in a learning cycle rather than factoring in early performances. If averaging is required by the district, grading expert Ken O'Connor (2003) recommends using "median"—not the "mean"—as the basis for arriving at a report card grade, in order to mitigate the potentially negative influence of poor early performance.

On a related note, principle 4 also challenges another grading practice—assigning "zeroes" to students who fail to turn in work on time or miss a test. The problem, of course, is that when a zero is averaged in, it distorts the achievement record. For example, a student may have learned the material well, but be downgraded for missed work and actually appear (according to the grade) to be lower achieving than another student who completed all her work but learned less. Although we certainly want to highlight the importance of dutiful work habits, averaging a zero into the achievement record is an imperfect solution. Here are alternatives to recording a zero in a grade book:

- assign an "I" for incomplete and allow the student to make up the work;
- for continued infractions, have the students stay in from recess or come to a Saturday session to complete their missed work; and/or

• document poor work habits under the *process* header, separate from the *performance* mark.

FORMATIVE ASSESSMENT AND FEEDBACK

As our assessment-planning framework reminds us, when we think about communicating assessment results, we need to be mindful of purpose and audience. Percentages, rubric scores, and letter grades may be appropriate ways of summarizing achievement on evaluative assessments for sharing with students, parents, administrators, and other schools. However, these symbols, by themselves, are not effective in support learning or improved performance. For those ends, we need more informative communications.

Unlike evaluative assessment, the purpose of formative assessments is feedback. To most effectively serve learning, feedback must meet several criteria (Wiggins, 2012):

1. Feedback must be timely. Waiting 2 weeks or more to find out how you did on a test or project will not help your learning. The delay in reporting results is one of the reasons that standardized accountability tests do not provide helpful feedback to teachers or learners—and that is not their primary purpose anyway.

2. Feedback must be specific and descriptive. Some teachers believe that they provide feedback when they give a score or grade. Not so! A "B," 83%, or 3 out of 4 on a rubric are simply symbols connoting some performance level, but these shorthand symbols fail the specificity test in that they do not convey *how* to improve. Effective feedback precisely describes strengths and weaknesses (e.g., "Your speech was well organized and your topic was interesting to the audience. However, you were speaking too softly in the beginning and rarely made eye contact with the audience.").

3. Feedback must be understandable to the receiver. Sometimes a teacher's comment or the language in a rubric is lost on a student. Using student-friendly language can make your feedback clearer and more comprehensible. For instance, instead of saying, "Document your reasoning process," a teacher could say, "Show each step in how you got your answer so others can follow your thinking."

4. Providing learners with timely and specific feedback is necessary but insufficient. Feedback must allow for adjustment on the student's part. Without opportunities for students to use the feedback, the benefits of formative assessment will remain unfulfilled—like chewing a meal without digesting! Indeed, research highlights this crucial component: "Feedback is most valuable when students have the opportunity to use it to revise their thinking as they are working on a unit or project" (Bransford et al., 2000, p. 129). Therefore, to get the most from formative assessments, we must schedule time for students to act on the feedback—that is, to practice, refine, redo, and revise.

McTighe and O'Connor (2005, p. 14) propose a straightforward test for a feedback system: "Can learners tell specifically from the given feedback what they have done well and what they could do next time to improve? If not, then the feedback is not specific or understandable enough for the learner."

CONCLUSION

In this chapter we have explored methods for communicating assessment results to various audiences for various purposes. We distinguished communication of evaluative assessment results from feedback on formative assessments. We proposed four principles that undergird effective grading practices and highlighted the characteristics of feedback for improving performance. In our next chapter, we will present specific ideas for teachers to improve the quality and impact of their classroom assessment practices. We will also offer tips to school leaders for enhancing the overall effectiveness of assessment in their schools.

Reflection Questions

- How do you currently communicate with students and their parents about academic performance, work habits, behavior, and so on? How effective are your communications?
- How do you compute report card grades and marks? Do you "average" student scores over time? Do you give "zeros" for missed work? If

so, how might you adjust your grading practices based on the ideas presented in this chapter?

- How does your school currently report student performance on report cards? Are separate factors (e.g., achievement, work habits, progress) reported independently? What changes in reporting might improve communications to parents and others?
- How do you provide your students with feedback? How do they make use of it? Are there ways that you can make your classroom feedback even more effective?
- How do you obtain feedback on your teaching that will help you improve your instruction?

Classroom Assessment Strategies for Teachers

Classroom assessments have the potential not only to measure learning but also to advance it. Here are seven classroom assessment practices that can help achieve that aim.

PRACTICE 1: USE ASSESSMENTS TO FRAME LEARNING GOALS

Effective teaching and learning begin with clear goals. In his book *Clarity in the Classroom* (2006), New Zealand educator Michael Absolum highlights the importance of task clarity and summarizes the benefits:

> For students to truly be able to take responsibility for their learning, both teachers and students need to be very clear about what is being learned, and how they should go about it. When learning and the path towards it are clear, research shows that there are a number of important shifts for students. Their motivation improves, they stay on task, their behavior improves, and they are able to take more responsibility for their learning. (p. 76)

Indeed, clarity about desired learning goals impacts all dimensions of the educational experience, including learning experiences, instructional resources, assessments, grades, and reports. For teachers, a careful consideration of the needed assessment evidence enhances goal clarity. It is one thing to identify a concept or skill as a learning goal; it is another to consider what assessment evidence will show that learners understand the concept or have proficiency in the skill. For example, if you want students to show an understanding of the concept of "supply and demand," how will you assess that goal? If the standards call for students to be able to construct and support an argument, how will you know that they have developed that capacity?

Having the assessments clearly in view informs and guides the instructional process necessary to equip students for expected performances. For students, goal clarity can positively affect their focus and motivation. Conversely, when the learning goals are unclear and the associated assessments are unknown, it is less likely that all learners will maintain focus, try their best, or persist when learning becomes challenging.

Teachers can post daily lesson objectives on a board to make lesson goals clear and identify "I can" statements that denote what students will be able to do when they have achieved targeted learnings at the end of a unit. We are simply proposing that teachers can go one step further and actually specify the evaluative assessments that will be used to gauge learning. By knowing what the culminating assessments will be, students are better able to focus on what the teachers expect them to learn, on what they will be expected to do with that knowledge, and how their work will be judged.

PRACTICE 2: DIAGNOSE BEFORE YOU START TEACHING

Like physicians or coaches, effective teachers don't just start teaching a unit before they have assessed their learners. Diagnostic assessment is as important to teachers as a physical exam is to doctors in prescribing an appropriate medical regimen. At the outset of any unit of study, it is possible that some students may have mastered some of the skills that the teacher is about to introduce, while others may already understand key concepts. Predictably, some learners will be deficient in prerequisite skills or harbor misconceptions about targeted concepts. Diagnostic assessments can reveal such variables that affect learning and should impact instruction.

Research evidence from cognitive psychology underpins the importance of using diagnostic assessments based on the critical role of prior knowledge in learning (Bransford et al., 2000).

> In the most general sense, the contemporary view of learning is that people construct new knowledge and understandings based on what they already know and believe . . .
>
> A logical extension of the view that new knowledge must be constructed from existing knowledge is that teachers need to pay attention to the incomplete understandings, the false beliefs, and the naïve renditions of concepts that learners bring with them to a given subject. (p. 10)

Diagnostic assessments need not be complex nor time consuming. We recommend using the most efficient methods—selected response or true–false formats to check for prior knowledge and uncover existing misconceptions, along with simple skill checks to assess students' proficiency levels for targeted skills. Armed with this diagnostic information, a teacher knows where to begin and what differentiation may be needed to address skill gaps or to allow advanced learners to move ahead.

PRACTICE 3: CREATE AN AUTHENTIC CONTEXT FOR PERFORMANCE-BASED ASSESSMENTS

As noted in Chapter 2, there are various types of learning goals that influence the forms of assessment used to gather evidence of their attainment. We proposed that when the goals focus on understanding and transfer, performance-based assessments will typically provide the most appropriate evidence of those goals. We highlighted the fact that effective performance assessment tasks need to engage students in two fundamental processes—applying their learning and providing explanations (e.g., showing their reasoning; supporting their inferences and solutions). We noted that the task should reveal students' abilities to transfer their learning—to use what they know in a new situation.

Now, we add one more recommendation: When using performance-based assessments, we encourage teachers to establish an authentic context for the tasks whenever possible. An authentic performance task elicits the application of knowledge and skills in a real-world manner, reflecting the ways people apply their learning in the world beyond the school. Such a task presents students with a realistic challenge, addresses a target audience, and calls for the development of genuine products and/or performances. The GRASPS acronym presented in Chapter 3 (Figure 3.4) offers a practical tool by which teachers and teams can design authentic tasks.

In line with our first recommendation above, presenting an authentic performance assessment task at the beginning of a new unit or course provides a relevant learning goal for students that helps them see a reason for their learning. Like the upcoming game in athletics, the play in theater, or the choral performance, authentic performance tasks are often motivating for learners and help them recognize the benefits of preparatory lessons, the equivalent of practices on the field or rehearsals on the stage. This is yet another way in which assessments can enhance learning, in addition to providing measures of it.

PRACTICE 4: SHOW EVALUATIVE CRITERIA IN THE BEGINNING

When open-ended assessments are used, evaluative judgments should be based on established criteria—and we strongly recommend that these criteria be shared with students early on. Students should not have to guess what is most important or wonder how their work will be judged. Assessment expert Richard Stiggins (1997) offers a useful aphorism that reminds us of the importance of making the success criteria public: "Students can hit any target that they can see and that holds still for them."

The implications of this principle are straightforward: Share the criterion lists and scoring rubrics that will be used for the evaluative assessments early on in a unit. Review the criteria with the students, and reference them regularly during instruction and as a part of formative assessment. When students know the evaluative criteria in advance, they have clear goals as they work. Thus, criteria become more than just the basis for evaluation; they provide clear performance targets, signaling to students what qualities should be present in their work. An additional benefit can be realized when teachers share performance criteria and rubrics with students—learners can use these tools for self- and peer assessment as they are working.

PRACTICE 5: PROVIDE ILLUSTRATIVE MODELS

Providing a criterion list or rubric to students in advance of an assessment is a worthwhile, but often insufficient, condition to support optimal learning and performance. Although experienced teachers usually have a clear conception of what they mean by "quality work," there is no guarantee that novice students will have the same understanding. Of course, it is helpful to share the evaluative criteria with them; however, that will not guarantee that they will necessarily know what the criteria mean. Phrases such as *insightful interpretation*, *logically organized*, and *sufficient evidence* may be lost on inexperienced students. We have found that learners are more likely to understand ongoing feedback and subsequent evaluations when teachers first show several examples that help translate the abstract language of evaluative criteria into more specific, concrete, and understandable terms. The principle here is straightforward: If we expect learners to produce high-quality work, they need to know what that looks like and how it differs from work of lesser quality.

Teachers may worry that students will simply copy or imitate a shown example. A related concern is that showing an excellent model (sometimes known as an exemplar) will dampen student creativity. We have found that by showing *multiple* models reflecting a range of performances, teachers can minimize these potential problems. When students can compare examples ranging in quality—from very strong to very weak—they are better able to internalize the differences. Similarly, when learners see how different students all achieved a high-level score, albeit in unique ways, they are less likely to imitate a single presented example. Moreover, by observing several examples and comparing them to their own work, students will become more able to accurately self-assess.

Another valuable use of models is to have students analyze them in order to induce the evaluative criteria. Here is a process: Present learners with a range of examples of work produced by students from previous years (with all names and other identifying information removed) and without any grades or scores attached. Then, have students work in small groups to review the samples, rank order them from best to worst, and describe the qualities that differentiate them. In so doing, students will be identifying the key traits and most salient performance qualities so that they will better understand evaluative criteria. This engaging process has proven to be one of the most productive methods for helping students really understand evaluative criteria.

Of course, if you would like to use this strategy, you'll need to collect examples of student work for use in future years. Obtain permission to use the work, and photocopy, photograph, or digitize it when necessary. If you work as part of a grade-level or department team, you can divide up the collection of student work on common assessments (e.g., team member 1 collects work samples for unit 1; member 2 collects work samples for unit 2). These can then be shared among the entire team. Note: For the low-level examples, we recommend that the teacher create those so as not to unwittingly embarrass any former student whose work might be recognizable.

PRACTICE 6: OFFER APPROPRIATE CHOICES

In Chapter 1, we presented the most frequent comments reported in the responses to the "best assessment" exercise (Figure 1.2), one of which was the "opportunity for some personal choice within assessments." This comment should not be surprising since we know that learners differ not only in how they prefer to take in and process information but also in how they best demonstrate their learning. Some students can communicate their learning clearly through writing; others prefer to provide oral explanations. Some students excel at creating visual products, while others can construct effective models. Consequently, a standardized, one-size-fits-all approach to classroom assessment may be efficient, but it is not always fair because any chosen format will favor some students and disadvantage others.

We have found that it is often possible for teachers to allow choices within assessments by which students can demonstrate their knowledge, skills, and understanding. Consider, for example, a health standard that calls for a basic understanding of a "balanced diet." Evidence of this goal could be obtained by having students explain the concept, present examples of balanced and unbalanced meals, and list health problems that might result from a nutritionally imbalanced diet. Such evidence could be collected in writing, but this requirement would be inappropriate for an ESL student with limited skills in written English or a learner with dysgraphia. Alternatively, students could be offered a few choices for responding, such as creating an illustrated brochure to show a balanced versus imbalanced diet or explaining the concept orally via a recorded podcast. As Grant Wiggins (1992) reminds us, we can have "standards without standardization."

In conjunction with our encouraging teachers to allow appropriate choices in assessments, we must also offer three cautionary notes:

1. If and when choices are allowed as part of a classroom
   assessment, they should always enable the collection of
   needed and appropriate evidence of learning based on
   targeted goals. For example, if an English/language arts
   standard calls for proficiency in writing, then students will
   need to write to show their learning; a visual or verbal
   response will not provide the evidence we need. However,
   we might offer the students some choice regarding the topic,
   audience, and/or form of the written product and still obtain
   the evidence we seek.

2. Any options offered must be manageable for the teacher and worth the time and energy of the student. It would be inefficient to have students develop an iMovie or a three-dimensional construction for assessing content that a multiple-choice test could easily assess.

3. Allowing some student choice(s) is generally most appropriate when using open-ended, performance-based assessments rather than for selected-response–type tests that generally seek a "correct" answer. However, when giving students choices on developing different types of products, be careful *not* to vary the evaluative criteria. It is important to recognize that evaluative criteria are derived primarily from the targeted learning goals/standards, rather than from the specific products of a given assessment task. This means that even when you offer students some choices in products or performances, the primary evaluative criteria should be the same. In other words, be careful to evaluate student work according to the most salient traits linked to the goal, rather than focusing only on the surface features of a particular product or performance (e.g., neatness, accurate spelling, creativity).

PRACTICE 7: PROVIDE ONGOING FEEDBACK

The legendary football coach, Vince Lombardi, reportedly said, "Feedback is the breakfast of champions." Indeed, all kinds of learning, whether on the practice field or in the classroom, benefit from feedback based on formative assessments. No winning coach waits until the big game to see how their team is doing. Indeed, the essence of coaching is giving continuous feedback to individual athletes and teams as they work to refine their skills and strategies during practices. Feedback during practice and scrimmages is the route to improved game performance in athletics, and the same principle applies to learning in the classroom. Indeed, an extensive base of educational research conclusively shows that the use of formative assessment and feedback yields one of the highest effects for significantly enhancing student achievement (Black & Wiliam, 1998; Hattie, 2008, 2012; Marzano, 2003).

Brookhart and McTighe (2019) recommend that formative assessment should be thought of not simply as a set of information-gathering techniques (e.g., an exit card, a nongraded quiz, a draft essay), but as an entire *cycle,* with the following aims:

Formative assessment benefits students and teachers alike. For students, formative assessment can preview learning targets, activate prior knowledge, spotlight success criteria, and offer ongoing feedback to help them improve their performance. For teachers, the information gleaned from pre- and ongoing assessments provides them with insights into their students' interests and preferred ways of learning, enables them to monitor learning along the way, and offers the feedback needed to guide instructional adjustments and differentiation. (p. 1)

The formative assessment learning cycle consists of the following elements to help learners:

1. understand the learning goals and associated "success criteria";
2. receive the helpful feedback that will enable them to recognize where they are in the learning process relative to the targeted goals and success criteria;
3. decide on specific actions and next steps needed to close the gap between their current level of learning and the success criteria; and
4. offer students the opportunity to implement the feedback and improve their products and performances.

In Chapter 5, we described the qualities of effective feedback: It must be timely, specific, and understandable to the receiver. We also noted that simply pinning a letter (B–) or a number (82%) on a student's work does not constitute feedback; neither do comments like "Nice job" or "You can do better." Although good grades and positive remarks may feel good, they do not advance learning.

We also reminded readers that students must be allowed time to use the feedback provided to make improvements—for example, to practice their skills or relearn material. As Jay and Steve can readily attest, writers rarely compose a perfect manuscript on the first try, which is why the writing process stresses cycles of drafting, feedback, and revision as the route to excellence.

PRACTICE 8: ENCOURAGE SELF-ASSESSMENT AND GOAL SETTING

Self-directed learners set personal learning goals, seek and use feedback to help them improve, self-assess their work, and make improvements independently, without having to wait for teachers to tell them what to do. Teachers can help cultivate these valuable learning habits by modeling goal setting and self-assessment, and by expecting students to apply these processes regularly and independently. The regular use of prompting questions such as the following signals to learners that self-assessment and goal setting are valued:

- What aspect of your learning/work was most effective?
- What aspect of your learning/work was not so effective?
- What specific actions can help improve your future learning/performance?
- What will you do differently next time?

By encouraging (and expecting) self-assessment and goal setting, teachers help learners become more effective at honest self-appraisal and constructive self-improvement. Over time, students should assume greater responsibility for enacting these processes independently.

Educators who provide regular opportunities for learners to self-assess and set goals often report a change in the classroom culture. As one teacher put it, "My students have shifted from asking, 'What did I get?' or 'What are you going to give me?' to becoming increasingly capable of knowing how they are doing and what they need to do to improve."

CONCLUSION

The eight strategies presented in this chapter have all been successfully employed by teachers in public, private, and international schools. We encourage you to share this chapter with members of your school leadership (or improvement) team, and make a commitment to try one or more of the suggested strategies. Leadership demands action!

Reflection Questions

- As a teacher, have you tried any of the eight strategies presented in this chapter? If so, how did it/they work?
- Self-assess your own assessment practices: Where are you most effective? In what areas do you need to improve? What actions will you take to make the needed changes?
- What advice or suggestions would you offer to a brand-new teacher to help them get the most from their classroom assessments?

CHAPTER 7

Tips for School Leaders

School leaders, including administrators, department chairs, grade-level leaders, and instructional coaches, can have a significant impact on learning in their schools. Given the influence that effective assessment practices can have on learning, it behooves all leaders to attend to this important element of our profession. Here are 10 tips for supporting impactful assessment in your school.

1. ASSESS THE STAFF

Effective teachers use diagnostic (pre-)assessments to check on the knowledge and skill levels of their students in order to determine the best instructional course. Similarly, school leaders can, and should, assess their teachers' understanding of the principles of sound assessment and their competency in applying effective practices in their classrooms. By gathering this information, a school's leadership team can target any professional development that may be needed to increase staff capacity to make optimum use of their assessments to enhance learning.

The Michigan Assessment Consortium publishes a set of Assessment Literacy Standards that can be used to generate observation tools and surveys to gauge the assessment knowledge and practices of a staff. You can access the document at https://www.michigan.gov/documents/mde/MAC_Asst_Literacy_Standards_1_601105_7.pdf.

2. CONDUCT A SCHOOL ASSESSMENT AUDIT

Collecting and analyzing evaluative assessments from the different grade levels and departments can provide a revealing profile of the assessment landscape of your school. You can form a faculty committee to review the collected assessment in terms of format, using the second page of our assessment-planning framework. For example, check to see what percentage of all evaluative assessments employ selected-response, brief constructed response, performance-based, or process-focused assessments? Analyze the assessments against Depth of Knowledge (DOK) or Bloom's Taxonomy to gauge their cognitive rigor. Examine the quality of associated criterion lists and rubrics. The results of your analysis can inform the need for targeted professional development to address any identified weaknesses (e.g., low-level test items, imbalance of assessment formats, grading of formative assessments, poor-quality rubrics).

Here is a description of a district assessment survey and associated analysis that can serve as a model: https://secureservercdn.net/198 .71.233.9/4ba.49d.myftpupload.com/wp-content/uploads/2020/11 /Donegal-Assessment-Survey-and-Analysis.pdf.

3. OFFER TARGETED PROFESSIONAL DEVELOPMENT

Based on the needs revealed by a staff diagnosis and/or an assessment audit, school leaders can organize professional learning sessions on topics related to classroom assessments, such as ones presented in this book. Workshop sessions can be offered by knowledgeable school/ district/service agency facilitators or external consultants. Professional development topics could include any of the following:

- Principles of quality assessments
- Effective use of diagnostic (pre-)assessments
- Effective use of formative assessments
- Strengths and limitations of various methods for evaluative assessment
- Designing and using performance-based assessments
- Designing and using criterion lists and rubrics
- Giving effective feedback to students
- Sound grading practices

Encourage staff to make a commitment to try at least one of the ideas presented in the workshop, and report on the results at the next staff/team meeting or professional learning session.

4. SHARE AND DISCUSS ASSESSMENT-RELATED ARTICLES AND BOOKS

Use a portion of faculty/team meetings and professional days to discuss articles on various aspects of assessment and grading. An article can be distributed to staff 2–3 days in advance with a few prompting questions such as those listed below. Discussions can then be framed by questions.

- Are we assessing everything we value or only the things that are easiest to test and grade?
- How do you use diagnostic assessments? What information do they provide, and how do you make use of it?
- How do you know if students really understand the content you are teaching? What assessments give you the best evidence of understanding?
- In what ways do you provide students with feedback? Which forms of feedback have proven most effective?
- How do you engage your students in the assessment process (e.g., working with them to identify "success criteria" for performance tasks; involving them in giving peer feedback to work in progress; when appropriate giving students "voice and choice" options on assessment tasks; encouraging them to self-assess their own work and set goals for future learning).
- What do you learn from the assessment results of your students? How does this information impact your teaching?

Here are some recommended articles that can be accessed online:

Black, P., & Wiliam, D. (1998). Inside the black box: Raising standards through classroom assessment. *Phi Delta Kappan, 80*(2), 139–144. https://weaeducation.typepad.co.uk/files/blackbox-1.pdf

Guskey, T. (2020). Breaking up the grade. *Educational Leadership, 78*(1), 40–46. http://www.ascd.org/publications/educational-leadership/sept20/vol78/num01/Breaking-Up-the-Grade.aspx

McTighe, J. (2018). Three key questions on measuring learning. *Educational Leadership, 75*(5), 14–20. http://www.ascd.org/publications/educational-leadership/feb18/vol75/num05/Three-Key-Questions-on-Measuring-Learning.aspx

Wiggins, G. (2012). Seven keys to effective feedback. *Educational Leadership, 70*(1), 10–16. http://www.ascd.org/publications/educational-leadership/sept12/vol70/num01/Seven-Keys-to-Effective-Feedback.aspx

In addition to reading and discussing short articles, school leaders can establish a voluntary book study using this book (or other assessment books). For example, have participants read a chapter a week and hold an in-person or virtual discussion session.

5. DEVELOP OR ADOPT PRINCIPLES OF ASSESSMENT AND GRADING

A set of principles provides a conceptual foundation on which effective classroom assessment and grading practices are grounded. Having such principles can serve as a touchstone for effective classroom assessments while offering a counterweight to ineffective practices habits that can impede optimal learning. They help define best assessment practices and depersonalize the feedback necessary to improve classroom assessments. Here are two recommended resources that can be used to generate a set of principles for assessment and grading:

Brookhart, S., Guskey, T., McTighe, J., & Wiliam, D. (2020). Eight essential principles for improving grading. *Educational Leadership*, *78*(1). http://www.ascd.org/publications/educational-leadership/sept20/vol78/num01/Eight-Essential-Principles-for-Improving-Grading.aspx

Shepard, L., Diaz-Biello, E., & Penuel, W. (2020). *Classroom assessment principles to support teaching and learning*. Center for Assessment, Design, Research and Evaluation, University of Colorado Boulder. https://www.colorado.edu/cadre/sites/default/files/attached-files/classroom_assessment_principles_to_support_teaching_and_learning_-_final_0.pdf

Once developed, school leaders can operationalize each of the principles in terms of observable practices. Figure 7.1 shows an example.

Figure 7.1. A Sample Chart of Assessment Principles and Practices

Assessment Principle	Assessment Practices
Assessments should align with goals.	Teachers use a variety of assessment methods to gather appropriate evidence of diverse learning goals.
Ongoing formative assessments provide feedback for improved learning.	Students regularly receive timely and specific feedback along with opportunities to use it to improve their learning and performance.

Then, school leaders can regularly review these principles and practices with staff. They can also use the indicators during classroom "walk-throughs" and for staff appraisals.

6. SHARE SUCCESSFUL PRACTICES

Take a few minutes at staff and team meetings to have teachers or teams share successful diagnostic, formative, and evaluative assessment practices that they (or their team) have tried. Discuss:

- What worked well? What challenges did you experience?
- What tips can you offer to other teachers who might want to try this?

Share high-quality performance assessment tasks as models. Discuss their qualities (e.g., open-ended, set in authentic contexts, involve "higher-order" thinking, allow students' "voice and choice").

Show examples of quality student work on performance tasks and projects that can spark fruitful discussions using question prompts, such as:

- Which learning goals are being assessed through this task/project?
- What evidence of learning is revealed in the student products/performances?
- By what criteria/rubric(s) was student work judged?
- To what extent were students engaged by the task/project?
- What strengths are evident in students' work? What patterns of weakness do we notice? How might we address these weak areas?
- What kind of instruction helped prepare learners to perform well on performance-based assessments?

7. SCHEDULE PEER VISITATIONS

Periodically, arrange for coverage for one or two periods so that teachers can visit classrooms of colleagues to observe effective implementation of assessment practices (e.g., students providing peer feedback to each other). Teachers are often more receptive to changing their assessment practices (for the better) when they can observe their colleagues using assessments effectively in "real" classrooms.

School leaders can employ various methods to enable peer visitations, including:

- Occasionally, ask secondary teachers to use their "free" period or elementary teachers to use a "special" (PE, art, music) as a time to visit and observe a colleague.
- Periodically, provide coverage for teachers by administrators, nonteaching specialists, student teachers, or substitutes.
- Hire one or more "roving" subs for a day to enable several teachers to visit other classrooms for 1–2 periods/time blocks.
- Occasionally, "double" up classes (e.g., one teacher takes two classes) to free up a grade-level or department colleague.
- Use special programs (e.g., a guest speaker in the auditorium) as an opportunity for peer visitations.

Carefully plan the peer visitations to ensure that there is a focus on a specific assessment practice. Following the visit, encourage the visiting staff member(s) to make a commitment to try one (or more) of the observed actions and report on the results at the next staff/team meeting.

8. DESIGN ASSESSMENTS COLLABORATIVELY

Engage grade level, department, and PLC teams in collaborating on assessment-related design work. It has been our experience that most teachers plan and deliver their instruction and associated assessments on their own. Although lesson or unit plans are sometimes reviewed by administrators or team/department leaders, teacher-developed assessments may never be scrutinized. The result can be weak or ineffective assessments. Teachers in the same school can be teaching to the *same* standards, yet be using wildly different assessments of those standards. Even when teachers have a high degree of assessment literacy, they can sometimes get too close to their work and fail to see any weaknesses. As an antidote to these potential problems, school leaders can encourage teams to work together to:

- develop common formative and evaluative assessments for the most important learning goals;

- develop common criterion lists and rubrics for performance-based assessments;
- serve as "critical friends" to review each other's assessments and provide helpful feedback.

Such collaborations are the hallmarks of professionalism and can result in tangible improvements in practice and concomitant gains in student learning.

9. EXAMINE ASSESSMENT RESULTS IN TEAMS

Educators are expected to use data as a basis for instructional decisionmaking and school planning. School and district administrators routinely dissect annual test score reports and summarize the results for teachers. Although results from an external test certainly provide useful data on student achievement, the review of a once-a-year "snapshot" is not sufficiently detailed nor timely enough to inform and guide continuous improvement actions at the classroom and school levels. As noted in Chapter 1, educators need a photo album of assessment information on *all* learning goals that matter, not just one picture of those things than can be cheaply tested on large-scale, standardized assessments. Accordingly, we recommend that teachers be actively involved as teams in analyzing student performance more frequently based on both formative and evaluative common assessments (McTighe, 2008). School improvement expert Mike Schmoker underscores this point: "Using the goals that they have established, teachers can meet regularly to improve their lessons and assess their progress using another important source: formative assessment data. Gathered every few weeks or at each grading period, formative data enable the team to gauge levels of success and to adjust their instructional efforts accordingly. Formative, collectively administered assessments enable teams to capture and celebrate short-term results, which are essential to success in any sphere" (2003, p. 22).

Improvement-oriented school leaders recognize the value of such collaborative work, and they structure the time and the expectations needed to enable grade level and department professional learning communities (PLCs) teams to review and evaluate student performance. To be most effective, PLCs need regularly scheduled meetings, common assessments and rubrics, and an established protocol for analyzing student work and interpreting the results. Wiggins and McTighe (2007) offer questions to guide a group's evaluation and analysis of student work and their planned adjustments to improve the results. The following URL offers a series of questions and a companion worksheet to use in this PLC process: http://jaymctighe.com/wordpress/wp-content /uploads/2013/06/Looking-at-Student-Work.pdf.

We have found that when teachers meet regularly in role-alike PLCs to evaluate assessment results, they begin to identify general *patterns* of strengths as well as areas needing improvement. Then, they combine their expertise to identify specific instructional interventions and resources that can address the weak areas. This approach is familiar to secondary teachers who coach team sports and sponsor extracurricular activities such as theater and band. As an example, football coaches often meet at someone's home or apartment to review game film from Saturday's game and *then* plan next week's practices based on their collective analysis of the team's weaknesses.

Let's apply the same process to academics. Such a professional learning process provides the fuel for continuous improvement while establishing a professionally enriching, results-oriented culture.

10. DISCOURAGE EXCESSIVE TEST PREP

Nearly all public schools and many independent and religious schools are assessed annually on external standardized tests—and the results matter. School and district test scores are frequently published in newspapers, school performances are compared and rated, and local real estate prices can even fluctuate based on the scores! High-performing schools are often given awards, while poor performance over time can result in public schools being placed on a state "watch list" or face a loss of accreditation, and school leaders in such schools may be transferred or demoted. In some states, teachers are evaluated based, in part, on student statewide assessment scores. Low test scores for private and charter schools may lead to enrollment declines and associated staff reductions.

It is not surprising, therefore, that administrators and teachers pay close attention to the results of these high-stakes assessments and strive to improve them. One impact of the concerns over external test scores is the increased use of test prep. Test prep refers to the use of class time to give students practice with the format of standardized tests, often through exercises and worksheets containing decontextualized, multiple-choice questions that mimic the test's format. Sometimes, test prep includes timed, on-demand, assessments to simulate test-day conditions. When computer-based testing is employed, students are often given opportunities to practice using a laptop or tablet device.

Although it certainly makes sense to familiarize students with the format of external accountability tests, we caution school leaders to avoid overemphasizing test prep. In our experience, a fixation on test prep can result in a narrowing of the curriculum and a crowding out of other assessment formats, especially performance-based and process-oriented assessments. McTighe (2018a) offers a cautionary note by likening practicing for a standardized test to raise the scores as akin to practicing for one's annual physical exam to become healthy! In other words, do not confuse the measures with the goals. The broad goal of schooling is to engage students in meaningful learning of important content. Students are rarely excited by a steady diet of multiple-choice worksheets compared to more authentic learning and assessment involving open-ended problems and issues, communicating for genuine purposes and audiences, conducting inquiries, and producing multimedia products. Like good nutrition, school leaders should promote a balanced approach to assessments that contribute to enduring learning that matters.

Here is a recommended article for school leaders (and maybe the entire school staff) that provides arguments against the overuse of test prep practices and recommends alternative approaches for deepening student learning and improving scores on external tests.

McTighe, J. (2017). *Beware of the test prep trap*. McTighe and Associates. https://secureservercdn.net/198.71.233.9/4ba.49d.myftpupload.com/wp-content/uploads/2020/10/Beware-of-Test-Prep-.pdf

CONCLUSION

The 10 tips described in this chapter have all been successfully employed by leaders in public, private, and international schools. We encourage you to share this chapter with members of your school leadership (or improvement) team, and make a commitment to try one or more of the suggested strategies. Leadership demands action!

Reflection Questions

- Have you tried any of the 10 tips presented in this chapter, whether targeting assessment or in conjunction with some other school initiative? If so, how did it/they work?
- What other ways might you support the growth of assessment literacy and practice in your staff?
- What advice would you offer to a brand-new school administrator, team leader, or department chair for improving the quality and effectiveness of assessments in their domain?
- How will you assess the impact of your assessment initiatives?

Glossary of Assessment Terms

analytic rubric/scoring: A scoring tool and associated procedure in which students' responses, products, or performances are evaluated according to specific elements or traits, with each receiving a separate score. For example, a piece of writing may be evaluated on several elements, such as idea development, organization, use of details, attention to audience, and language usage and mechanics. Analytic scores may be weighted and totaled. (See *holistic/rubric scoring.*)

anchor(s): Representative responses, products, or performances used to illustrate each point on a scoring scale. They are also referred to as models. Anchors for the highest score point are sometimes referred to as exemplars.

assessment: Any systematic basis for making inferences about characteristics of people, usually based on various sources of evidence; the global process of synthesizing information about individuals in order to understand and describe them better (Brown, 1983).

authentic assessment: Refers to assessment tasks that are set in genuine contexts and evoke demonstrations of knowledge and skills in ways that they are applied in the larger world beyond the school. A related connotation of the term has to do with the extent to which a task reflects the interests and experiences of students.

bias: Factors that interfere with a valid inference regarding a student's knowledge and skill. For example, an English language learner (ELL) student may know the science content but not be able to read the test items in English.

competency: A goal statement specifying the ability to do something successfully or efficiently; hence a competency refers to the demonstration of skills and processes or the ability to apply learning.

constructed-response item: A test item format that requires students to generate a response to a prompt (e.g., a question, problem, reading passage, graphic). Generally, the response to these item types are brief (e.g., fill-in-the-blank, short answer, show your work, a Tweet). (See *performance-based assessment; selected-response item*.)

content standard: A goal statement specifying desired knowledge, skills or processes, and attitudes to be developed as a result of educational experiences. (See *performance standard*.)

criteria: Guidelines, rules, or principles by which student responses, products, or performances are evaluated.

criterion list: An evaluation tool consisting of designated criteria, but without descriptive details. Unlike a rubric, a performance list merely provides a set of features without defining the terms or describing varying degrees of quality or proficiency.

criterion referenced: An approach for describing a student's performance on an assessment according to established criteria. (See *norm referenced*.)

developmental scale: Describes growth along a proficiency continuum, ranging from novice to expert (e.g., the colored belts in karate that designate various proficiency levels). Longitudinal rubrics are well suited to subjects that emphasize skill performance. Hence, they are natural to English language arts, physical education, the arts, and language acquisition. (Also known as proficiency scales or developmental rubric.)

diagnostic assessment: A form of preassessment used to identify students' strengths, weaknesses, prior knowledge, and skill levels before beginning new instruction. (See *evaluative assessment; formative assessment; preassessment*.)

disposition: A quality of character or a tendency to act in a specified way. Examples include persistence, open-mindedness, and seeking clarity. (See *habits of mind*.)

evaluation: Judgment regarding the quality, value, or worth of a response, product, or performance based on established criteria.

evaluative assessment: Assessment measures that result in a final score or grade. (See *diagnostic assessment; formative assessment; summative assessment*).

formative assessment: Ongoing, diagnostic assessment providing information (feedback) to guide instruction and improve student performance. Formative assessments are for the purpose of *informing* learners and teachers, not for evaluating. Thus, results of these assessments should not be graded. (See *summative assessment.*)

generalizability: The extent to which responses, products, or performances that are sampled by a set of assessment activities are representative of the broader domain being assessed.

habits of mind: Dispositions that intelligent individuals utilize when faced with challenging problems or questions to which the answer is not readily known. (See *disposition.*)

high-stakes assessment: An assessment may be labeled "high stakes" if there are notable consequences based on the results. Standardized accountability tests are often considered high stakes for districts and schools if their results influence ratings, educational funding, accreditation, property values in a community, or impact professional staff positions. For students, their performance on a high-stakes assessment could impact consequential decisions such as promotion, graduation, admission, certification, evaluation, or awards. For example, a minimum competency exam would be considered high stakes for students if passing the exam was necessary to receive a high school diploma. (See *standardized assessment.*)

holistic rubric/scoring: A scoring tool and associated procedure yielding a single score based on an overall impression of a response, product, or performance. (See *analytic/rubric scoring.*)

indicator: A specific description of an outcome in terms of observable and assessable behaviors. An indicator specifies what a person who possesses the qualities articulated in an educational outcome knows, understands, and can do.

interdisciplinary or integrated assessment: An assessment that appraises students' abilities to apply concepts, principles, skills, and processes from two or more disciplines to a central question, theme, issue, or problem. Interdisciplinary assessments may also be used to assess transdisciplinary outcomes such as critical thinking, creativity, communication via various media, and collaboration.

norm referenced: An approach for describing a student's performance on an assessment in comparison to a norm group. (See *criterion referenced.*)

performance-based assessment (also known as performance assessment or performance task): An assessment activity that requires students to construct a response, create a product, or perform a demonstration to demonstrate or apply their learning. Performance-based assessments generally do not yield a single correct answer or solution but allow for a wider range of responses. Thus, evaluations of student responses, products, and performances are based on judgments guided by criteria. (See *authentic assessment; performance task.*)

performance standard: An established level of achievement, quality, or proficiency. Performance standards set expectations about how much students should know and how well they should perform.

performance task: An assessment activity, or set of activities, that elicits one or more responses to a question or problem. (See *authentic assessment; performance-based assessment.*)

portfolio: A purposeful, integrated collection of student work showing effort, progress, or achievement in one or more areas. Since they feature works selected over time, portfolios are well suited to assess student growth and development.

preassessment: An assessment used at the beginning of new instruction to determine the optimal starting point based on students' prior knowledge and skill levels. A comparable assessment may be given postinstruction to determine the extent to which students have achieved the targeted learning. (See *diagnostic assessment.*)

proficiency: Having or demonstrating a high degree of skill in a particular area.

reliability: The degree to which an assessment yields dependable and consistent results across raters, over time, or across different versions of the same assessment. (See *validity.*)

rubric: A scoring tool used to evaluate a student's performance in a content area. Rubrics consist of a fixed measurement scale (e.g., a 4-point scale) and a list of criteria that describes the characteristics of products or performances for each score point. Rubrics are frequently accompanied by examples (anchors) of responses, products, or performances to illustrate each of the points on the scale. (See *analytic rubric/scoring; holistic rubric/scoring; rubric.*)

selected-response item: A test item format that presents learners with a prompt (e.g., a question, problem, reading passage, graphic) and a set of selectable options. Students choose from among the given alternatives rather than generating their own response.

Familiar selected-response formats are multiple-choice, true–false, and matching. Since selected-response items are generally constructed with a "right" or best answer in mind, they can quickly be scored using an electronic scanning device or an answer key. (See *constructed-response item; performance-based assessment*.)

single-point rubric: A tool consisting of a list of criteria related to a student's performance. A single-point rubric typically consists of three columns. The criteria are presented in the center column. The column on the left side contains boxes to note areas needing improvement for each criterion. The column on the right side contains boxes where strengths or successes can be noted. Technically, a single-point rubric is misnamed since it does not contain a performance scale describing the characteristics of products or performances for the various score points in the scales. Nonetheless, it is a useful tool for formative assessment. (See *analytic rubric/scoring; holistic rubric/scoring; rubric*.)

standardized assessment: An assessment that uses a set of consistent procedures for constructing, administering, and scoring. The goal of standardization is that all students are assessed under uniform conditions so that interpretation of their performance is comparable and not influenced by differing conditions (Brown, 1983).

summative assessment: Culminating assessment for a unit, grade level, or course of study used for evaluating the degree of mastery or proficiency according to identified content standards. Unlike formative assessments, the results of summative assessments are typically evaluated and reported (e.g., as a grade or percentage). Note: We have chosen to use the term *evaluative assessment* in this book.

test: A set of questions or situations designed to elicit responses that permit an inference about what a student knows or can do. Tests generally occur within established time limits, restrict access to resources (e.g., reference materials), and yield a limited range of acceptable responses.

validity: Refers to the degree to which an assessment measures what it is intended to measure. More precisely, the term determines the extent to which the results from any assessment enable valid inferences to be made about a student's knowledge or proficiency.

References

Absolum, M. (2006). *Clarity in the classroom* (p. 26). Hodder Education.

American Educational Research Association, American Psychological Association, National Council on Measurement in Education, & Joint Committee on Standards for Educational and Psychological Testing (U.S.). (2014). *Standards for educational and psychological testing.* American Educational Research Association.

Arter, J., & McTighe, J. (2001). *Scoring rubrics in the classroom: Using performance criteria for assessing and improving student performance.* Corwin Press.

Black, P., & Wiliam, D. (1998). Inside the black box: Raising standards through classroom assessment. *Phi Delta Kappan, 80*(2), 139–144.

Bransford, J. D., Brown, A. L., & Cocking, R. R., (Eds.). (2000). *How people learn: Brain, mind, experience, and school.* National Academies Press.

Brookhart, S., Guskey, T., McTighe, J., & Wiliam, D. (2020). Eight essential principles for improving grading. *Educational Leadership, 78*(1).

Brookhart, S., & McTighe, J. (2019). *The formative assessment learning cycle: A quick reference guide* (p. 1). ASCD.

Brookhart, S., Stiggins, R., McTighe, J., & Wiliam, D. (2019). *The future of assessment practices: Comprehensive and balanced assessment systems.* Learning Sciences International.

Brookhart, S. M., & Nitko, A. J. (2019). *Educational assessment of students* (8th ed.). Pearson.

Brown, F. (1983). *Principles of educational and psychological testing* (3rd ed.). Holt, Rinehart and Winston.

CASEL. *SEL is. . . .* Collaborative for Academic, Social, and Emotional Learning (CASEL). https://casel.org/what-is-sel

CTB/McGraw-Hill. (2010). *A guide for effective assessment.* https://www.peoria publicschools.org/Page/14206

Darling-Hammond, L., & Adamson, F. (2013, June). The next generation of assessments can—and must—be better. *ASCD Express, 8*(18).

Ferrara, S., Goldberg, G., & McTighe, J. (1995, April). *Ways in which teachers communicate learning targets, criteria, and standards for performance to their students.* Paper presented at the annual meeting of the American Educational Research Association, San Francisco.

Gareis, C., & Grant, L. (2015). *Teacher-made assessments: How to connect curriculum, instruction, and student learning* (2nd ed.). Routledge.

Gonzales, J. (2015). Meet the single point rubric. *Cult of pedagogy* (blog post). https://www.cultofpedagogy.com/single-point-rubric

Guskey, T. (2020a). Breaking up the grade. *Educational Leadership, 78*(1), 40–46.

Guskey, T. (2020b). *Get set. Go: Creating effective grading and reporting systems.* Solution Tree.

Hattie, J. (2008). *Visible learning: A synthesis of over 800 meta-analyses relating to achievement.* Routledge.

Hattie, J. (2012). *Visible learning for teachers: Maximizing impact on learning.* Routledge.

Marzano, R. (2003). *What works in schools: Translating research into action.* ASCD.

McMillan, J. H. (2014). *Classroom assessment: Principles and practice for effective standards-based instruction* (6th ed.). Pearson.

McTighe, J. (2008). Making the most of professional learning communities. *The Learning Principal, 3*(8), 1–7. https://www.ceelcenter.org/wordpress/wpcontent/uploads/2016/06/Making_the_Most_of_PLCs.pdf

McTighe, J. (2013). *Core learning: Assessing what matters most.* School Improvement Network.

McTighe, J. (2018a). Three key questions on measuring learning. *Educational Leadership, 75*(5), 18–19.

McTighe, J. (2018b). *Beware of the test prep trap.* McTighe and Associates. https://secureservercdn.net/198.71.233.9/4ba.49d.myftpupload.com/wp-content/uploads/2020/10/Beware-of-Test-Prep-.pdf

McTighe, J., & Ferrara, S. (1998). *Assessing learning in the classroom.* National Education Association.

McTighe, J., & O'Connor, K. (2005). Seven practices for effective learning. *Educational Leadership, 63*(3), 10–17.

McTighe, J., & Wiggins, G. (2004). *The understanding by design professional development workbook* (p. 233). ASCD.

Michigan Assessment Consortium. (2005). *Assessment literacy standards: A national imperative.* https://www.michigan.gov/documents/mde/MAC_Asst_Literacy_Standards_1_601105_7.pdf

National Core Arts Standards State Education Agency Directors of Arts Education. (2014). *National core arts standards.* State Education Agency Directors of Arts Education.

National Council for the Social Studies (NCSS). (2013). *The college, career, and civic life (C3) framework for social studies state standards: Guidance for enhancing the rigor of K–12 civics, economics, geography, and history.* NCSS.

National Governors Association Center for Best Practices & Council of Chief State School Officers. (2010a). *Common core state standards for mathematics.* Authors.

National Governors Association Center for Best Practices & Council of Chief State School Officers. (2010b). *Common core state standards for English language arts.* Authors.

NGSS Lead States. (2013). *Next generation science standards: For states, by states.* National Academies Press.

Niguidula, D. (2005, November). Documenting learning with digital portfolios. *Educational Leadership, 63*(3), 44–47.

Niguidula, D. (2019). *Demonstrating student mastery with digital badges and portfolios.* ASCD.

O'Connor, K. (2018). *How to grade for learning, K–12* (4th ed.). Corwin.

Popham, W. J. (2013). *Classroom assessment: What teachers need to know* (7th ed.). Pearson.

Schmoker, M. (2003, February). First things first: Demystifying data analysis. *Educational Leadership, 60*(5), 22.

Shepard, L., Diaz-Biello, E., & Penuel, W. (2020). *Classroom assessment principles to support teaching and learning.* Center for Assessment, Design, Research and Evaluation, University of Colorado Boulder. https://www .colorado.edu/cadre/sites/default/files/attached-files/classroom_assess ment_principles_to_support_teaching_and_learning_-_final_0.pdf

Stiggins, R. (1997). *Student-centered classroom assessment* (2nd ed.). Macmillan.

Stiggins, R. (2004). *Student-involved assessment for learning.* Pearson.

Stiggins, R. J., & Conklin, N. F. (1992). *In teachers' hands.* State University of New York Press.

Stiggins, R., & Duke, D. (2008). Effective instructional leadership requires assessment leadership. *Phi Delta Kappan, 90*(4), 285–291.

Tomlinson, C., & McTighe, J. (2006). *Differentiated instruction and understanding by design* (p. 132). ASCD.

Wiggins, G. (1989). A true test: Toward more authentic and equitable assessment. *The Phi Delta Kappan, 70*(9), 703–713.

Wiggins, G. (1992). Standards, not standardization: Evoking quality student work. *Educational Leadership, 4*(5), 18–25.

Wiggins, G. (1998). *Educative assessment: Designing assessments to inform and improve student performance.* Jossey-Bass Publishers.

Wiggins, G. (2012). Seven keys to effective feedback. *Educational Leadership, 70*(1), 10–16.

Wiggins, G., & McTighe, J. (2004). *Understanding by design* (Expanded 2nd ed.). ASCD.

Wiggins, G., & McTighe, J. (2007). *Schooling by design: Mission, action, and achievement.* ASCD.

Wiggins, G., & McTighe, J. (2011). *The understanding by design guide to creating high quality units.* ASCD.

Wiggins, G., & McTighe, J. (2012). *The understanding by design advanced guide to advanced concepts in creating and reviewing units.* ASCD.

Index

About the Authors

Jay McTighe is an accomplished author, having coauthored 17 books, including the award-winning and best-selling *Understanding by Design* series with Grant Wiggins. His books have been translated into 14 languages. Jay has also written more than 50 book chapters, articles, and blogs, and has been published in leading journals, including *Educational Leadership* (ASCD) and *Education Week*. Jay has an extensive background in professional development and is a regular speaker at state, national, and international conferences and workshops.

Steve Ferrara is a professional psychometrician who works for Cognia. He has worked on more than 20 state accountability testing programs for grade-level students, students with significant cognitive disabilities, and English learners, and on interim and formative assessment products. As state director of student assessment in Maryland (1985–1997), he worked extensively with classroom teachers, principals, and curriculum directors on state and classroom assessment practices. Steve has published over 50 professional journal articles and book chapters and has written more than 200 conference papers and presentations. He started his career as a high school special education teacher after spending a year as a Head Start teacher.